D0168373

"Hans' book is a leader's mirror ... you'll see yourself in previously unrevealed ways and learn what it takes to 'get presentable' for effective leadership for His glory."

**Joseph M. Stowell,** President, Moody Bible Institute

"This is one of the most practical books on leadership I have in my own personal library. If you are serious about becoming a better leader, you will want to read this book."

**John C. Maxwell,** Author, Speaker, and Founder
The INJOY Group

"Solid concepts. Great quotes. Good stories. Hans Finzel has combined sophisticated leadership theory with practical principles to teach us how to lead. Read this book today and become a better leader tomorrow."

**Leith Anderson,** Pastor, Wooddale Church,
Eden Prairie, Minnesota

"I think that chapter 5, 'The Absence of Affirmation,' is worth the price of the book. Leaders today desperately need to learn how to affirm followers and emerging leaders."

**Bobby Clinton,** Professor of Leadership,
Fuller Theological Seminary

"*A must-have book. From my experience in multi-ministry environments over recent years, the content of this book is the fabric that leaders need for these days.*"

**Luis Bush,** International Director,
AD2000 & Beyond Movement

"*Easy to read and practical, yet authoritative and experience based. A great addition to the library of anyone in leadership.*"

**Robertson McQuilken,** President Emeritus,
Columbia International University

"*Thank you, Hans, for not just giving us 'servant-leadership' language, but showing us how to be servant-leaders. And you have done it in a wonderfully appealing way. As we avoid the ten 'minefields' you have outlined, we will become leaders of integrity and authenticity.*"

**Crawford W. Loritts, Jr.,** Author, Speaker,
Associate U.S. Director, Campus Crusade for Christ

"*This easy-to-read presentation by Hans Finzel is a great reminder to every leader of the most important mistakes to avoid. It will be invaluable to those just assuming new responsibilities.*"

**Paul Eshleman,** Director, The JESUS Film Project

# The Top Ten Mistakes Leaders Make

## HANS FINZEL

Building the New Generation of Believers

An Imprint of Cook Communications Ministries
COLORADO SPRINGS, COLORADO • PARIS, ONTARIO
KINGSWAY COMMUNICATIONS, LTD., EASTBOURNE, ENGLAND

NexGen® is an imprint of
Cook Communications Ministries, Colorado Springs, CO 80918
Cook Communications, Paris, Ontario
Kingsway Communications, Eastbourne, England

THE TOP TEN MISTAKES LEADERS MAKE
© 1994, 2000 by Hans Finzel.

All rights reserved. No part of this book may be reproduced without written permission, except for brief quotations in books and critical reviews. For information, write Cook Communications Ministries, 4050 Lee Vance View, Colorado Springs, CO 80918.

Printed in the UNITED STATES OF AMERICA
5 6 7 8 9 Printing/Year 08 07 06 05 04

Cover Design: Smith/Lane Associates
Cover Photo: Ken Tannenbaum/Image Bank
Copyediting: Bill Deckard, Barbara Williams

Unless otherwise indicated, all Scripture quotations are taken from the HOLY BIBLE, NEW INTERNATIONAL VERSION®. NIV®. Copyright © 1973, 1978, 1984 by International Bible Society. Used by permission of Zondervan Publishing House. All rights reserved. Other references are from the NEW AMERICAN STANDARD BIBLE (NASB). Copyright © The Lockman Foundation 1960, 1962, 1963, 1968, 1971, 1972, 1973, 1975, 1977, 1995. Used by permission.

**Library of Congress Catalog-in-Publication Data**

Finzel, Hans.
  The top ten mistakes leaders make / by Hans Finzel.
    p. cm.
  Includes bibliographical references.
  ISBN 1-56476-246-7
  1. Leadership.    2.Executive ability.    I. Title
HD57.7F56   1994
658.4'092—dc20                              93-46109
                                                CIP

# CONTENTS

# Dedicated

to my four children

Mark
Jeremy
Cambria
Andrew

It is you — bar none — that I care most
to lead in the best way possible
by the grace of God

# ACKNOWLEDGMENTS

One of my first big leadership roles was with our Boy Scout troop as a young Eagle Scout. Then, through my teen years of working at various jobs, I often seemed to end up in leadership roles. One that stands out is a job I fell into that never ceases to amaze me: At age fifteen I was the head cook on the night shift at a Shoney's restaurant.

Through my subsequent two decades of experience in leadership, I managed to avoid by default any formal training in the area. All that changed in 1986 when I met Sam Metcalf, president of Church Resource Ministries of Fullerton, California (who has become one of my mentors — see chap. 9). Sam told me about an unusual professor at the Fuller School of World Mission in Pasadena, who was pioneering an innovative approach to leadership study for Christian leaders. I flew to California to meet this unique gentleman and was sold on his approach to leadership training. By September 1987 I was deeply submerged in my doctoral studies under the mentorship of this colorful individual, Bobby Clinton. Clinton has done more than anyone to revolutionize my view of leadership, and to put me on track for what I believe to be biblical leadership values that will serve me well into the twenty-first century.

I must also acknowledge the unbelievable support of my wife, Donna. For almost two decades she has put up with my bursts of energy that get me overextended amid the chaos of an already busy life and heavy responsibilities. The last two books I have written are good examples. The timing of both could not have been worse. My book on baby boomers (Victor Books, 1989) was written during the first six months of our twins' lives, while I was in my doctoral studies. Two other young sons were already in our home needing our attention. This book you hold in your hands I committed to write before being selected to the leadership role I now fill in a global enterprise that has consumed most of my attention since I took over. I appreciate how many nights and weekends away from home Donna allowed me, to complete this project which was so important to me. My leadership is *our* leadership. Anything I have learned or done of value in these years I share in partnership with the great wife God has graciously given me.

# INTRODUCTION

The setting was a stuffy, windowless conference room at the local Holiday Inn. Hot, tired, and weary, we were nearing the end of a marathon day of intense scrutiny as my wife, Donna, and I were meeting with our organization's CEO search committee. I was their main candidate for becoming the new CEO, and they wanted to make sure that no stones were left unturned in their homework. This all-day session was the culmination of their six-month investigation into my background. I felt many of the same emotions people who submit themselves to the searchlight intensity of Senate confirmation hearings must feel.

One of the gentlemen on my left asked me a question which surprised me: "Hans, tell us why you want to become our new leader."

To put this question in perspective, our organization is a global concern. We have a presence in more than forty areas of the world, with an overseas personnel force of more than 700 workers. In addition, there is our home office here in the United States with a staff of more than fifty, and six regional offices throughout North America.

"Did I ever *say* I wanted to become the leader?" I answered with a big smile. "You never heard that from my lips!" I went on to explain that I had always been willing, each step along the way, to accept larger responsibilities during my twelve-year tenure in the organization. And now I was willing to take the top job, "But be very clear that I am *willing*, not seeking."

I knew that this career move would bring tremendous pressure into my life, my marriage, and my young family. And now that I have been in the role for some time, I've got bad news for you aspiring leaders out there: It is a lot more intense than I ever imagined!

Leadership is dangerous. World history can best be written by studying the lives of great and terrible leaders and what they accomplished through others. We who are in leadership can on the one hand move men, women, and mountains for tremendous good. At the same time, we hold in our hands the power to do irreparable damage to our followers by the mistakes we make.

The greater our sphere of leadership influence, the more our impact on the world around us. And the more people we lead, the greater the potential damage caused through our poor decisions and actions. This is one of the sobering realities we must face when we take up the mantle of leadership.

Good leaders seem to be a scarce commodity today. There are plenty of openings but fewer and fewer good candidates.

Why is it that so many organizations, churches, and schools are looking for leaders to fill empty slots? Perhaps the problem is not really that new:

I searched for a man among them who should . . .
stand in the gap before Me for the land, that I should
not destroy it; but I found no one (Ezek. 22:30).

This book is not intended to answer the question of leadership scarcity, but rather to look at what makes a good leader go bad, or better yet, what habits to avoid if you want to help fill the gap and replenish the great leadership famine.

My informal survey of leaders suggests that people fall into leadership more by accident than by design. Through whatever circumstances led them to that point, they are thrown into leadership and become what I call "reluctant leaders." How many actually sign up or apply for leadership positions? It is the kind of role you are chosen for—you usually cannot volunteer.

After falling into leadership, we tend to do what comes naturally—we "wing it." And that's what gets leaders into trouble, because good leadership practice is often the opposite of conventional wisdom. It may come naturally, for instance, to treat employees like children, but it is best to treat them with adult respect—as your most precious resource for success.

Few prepare themselves or volunteer for leadership. It is a calling for the appointed. This seems to be true across the board—in industry, business, and government. And it is equally true if not more true in ministry vocations. Many people who come into positions of leadership in churches or Christian organizations have little or no training in leadership and management. Leaders of Christian enterprises tend to be spiritually qualified but often organizationally illiterate. The problem is, leadership requires both the heart and the head.

The greatest lessons I've personally learned about good leadership have been through my own mistakes. And from bad examples. Those mistakes and bad examples have helped identify some common patterns in the mistakes leaders tend to make.

So what are the most common pitfalls of leadership? And, can we really learn any good lessons from the bad mistakes of others?

## Learning Good from Things that Go Bad

Not too many years ago my own professional career came to a screeching halt as I fell into a deep, black pit of burnout. The situation stemmed largely from my relationship with the leader above me. I had finished college and graduate school to prepare myself for a successful career in my chosen field. My heart was filled with dreams and visions of how I would make a difference in the world. *Look out world, here I come!* Through my efforts, a few good things began to be accomplished. I was involved with an exciting new venture that was really making a difference.

My professional track record was about to be derailed, and I never saw it coming. Great leaders challenge people to attempt things they would never try on their own. I met a man who inspired me and chal-

> **Great leaders inspire us to go places we would never go on our own, and to attempt things we never thought we had in us.**

lenged me to a great cause. He recruited me with promises of great things to come. I was going to be part of something so much larger than I had ever dreamed of. My wife and I moved to join his team, and the first few years were excellent. Great leaders do that. They inspire us to go places we would never go on our own, and to attempt things we never have thought we had in us.

Then it happened. At the five-year marker under his leadership, things began to unravel. He lost confidence in me and I in him. Suddenly my world came crashing down around me. Those youthful hopes and early dreams were dashed like waves crashing against ugly, jagged rocks. I lost sight of the future as I fell deep into a valley of depression. My heart, once filled with zeal to do good in a bad world, was suddenly filled with bitterness. I was angry, and that anger arose out of my frustration over broken dreams and unfulfilled promises.

And who was the main cause of my blame? I would be

arrogant not to take the blame myself. I was at fault for failing to learn some important lessons on leadership. God was lowering my pride a few hundred notches, and teaching me much about my own leadership shortcomings. More about those lessons later in this book.

Then there was my leader. A great leader with some equally great shortcomings. I fell from such heights of promise to such depths of despair in part because of his actions — and in some cases because of his neglect of action toward me. This leader, like most, had no clue as to how much power he wielded over his subordinates. Great leaders forget what it feels like to be led. Some have never even experienced "followership," because they have led from the moment they were born — right out of the womb, bossing Mom and Dad around!

Leaders have incredible power for good or ill in people's lives. A few control the destiny of many. But how many of us start out with lofty ideals and dreams, only to be soured by our experience with leaders? Before we know it, people lose trust and the trench warfare begins. Or, nothing is said but confidence in our leadership begins to erode quickly. People resign and walk. Leaders are fired. Division, strife, and backbiting reign. The work, whatever it is, is slowed, damaged, or comes to a screeching halt.

## Leadership Is *Influence*

The subject of leadership can be very confusing. If you should ask me to recommend one good book on leadership, I would probably pause and draw a blank. It's not that I don't have many good books on the subject. It's just that they emphasize so many various nuances of the subject. I would ask you what area of leadership you want to read about. One of my top ten favorite general books on the qualities of great leadership is *Leaders,* by Warren Bennis and Burt Nanus. They begin by relating the frustrating history of research into the true nature of great leadership.

Decades of academic analysis have given us more than 350 definitions of leadership. Never have so many labored so long to say so little. Like love, leadership continued to be something everyone knew existed but nobody could define. Many other theories of leadership have come and gone. Some looked at the leader. Some looked at the situation. None has stood the test of time. With such a track record, it is understandable why leadership research and theory have been so frustrating as to deserve the label "the La Brea Tar Pits" of organizational inquiry. Located in Los Angeles, these asphalt pits house the remains of a long sequence of prehistoric animals that came to investigate but never left the area (Bennis & Nanus, 1985: 4–6).

I tend to view the profound process of leadership in terms of a very simple definition: Leadership is *influence.* That's it. A one-word definition. Anyone who *influences* someone else to do something has *led* that person.

> **How Do You Spell Leadership?**
> **I-n-f-l-u-e-n-c-e**

Another definition might be, *A leader takes people where they would never go on their own.*

### Do Most Leaders Just Wing It?

Years have passed since my experience with leadership gone bad. I have forgiven that leader. In fact to this day I admire him for the great leadership gifts he has. And I thank him for all he contributed to my life in our years together. He is what I would call a born leader. He inspired me to greatness. He helped me in countless ways. And hopefully I have learned from his mistakes.

What makes leaders fail? Why are bad leadership habits perpetuated? *Because most of us who lead have neither been formally trained nor had good role models.* So we lead as we were led. We wing it.

At a recent conference of Christian pastors and leaders, the question was raised, "How many of you ever had one course in college or seminary on how to lead effectively?" The results were shocking. Almost no one had had any formal training. Lacking any training, leaders lead as they were led. They may be extensively trained in how to do ministry, but not in how *to lead* others who minister. Seminaries rarely offer such training. Churches don't do a very good job of it either. It is left to books, seminars, tapes, and other nonformal sources of training to build the leader's knowledge of skills in leadership.

The average leader faces at least five problems in learning to lead, each of which will be addressed with solutions in this book:

1. *Today's leaders replicate the poor leadership habits they have observed in others.* We will describe how we imitate what we see modeled.
2. *Today's leaders often lack basic skills for common leadership demands.* We will look at some positive skills and attitudes that can overcome the "top ten mistakes" which I will present.
3. *Today's leaders lack good models and mentoring.* I will illustrate positive leadership values with some real-life examples of good leaders.
4. *Today's leaders lack formal training in leadership.* Since formal training is usually not available for the busy leader, this book offers practical insight that he or she can use.

---

**Why Do New Leaders Often Get a Bad Startup?**

- We replicate the poor leadership habits of others.
- We aren't born with leadership skills.
- We lack good models and mentors.
- We lack formal training.
- We suffer confusion over the secular versus the spiritual in leadership philosophy.

---

5. *Today's leaders suffer confusion over the conflict between secular and biblical leadership values.* An important underpinning of my approach is to highlight the contrast between what the Bible values in leadership (the best example of good leadership is Jesus Christ and His servanthood approach) and what secular leadership models (all too often, top-down control).

This book is for those of you who find yourselves called to lead and are a bit apprehensive about blowing it. The insights in these pages apply whether you are leading a company, a ministry, a department, one or two coworkers, a Girl Scout club, an army platoon, a committee, or your family.

As baby boomers and busters come into positions of leadership across the land, a whole new hunger for practical leadership wisdom is emerging. We the younger generations are being called on to lead everything from Fortune 500 companies and family businesses to churches, seminaries, missions, factories, and even the U.S. government. Consider this book a Boomer Bible on how to lead.

Top-flight leaders really aren't born, they learn by trial and error. Poor leadership habits and practices can spawn new generations of poor leaders. Or, they can create enough discomfort that the leader figures out how to do it right. That has been my own experience, and I offer the notes from my journey to others who are called to lead.

I enjoy stealing away from the pressures of my work to take my four children biking down the Illinois Prairie Path not far from our home. As the dad, it is usually in my hands to determine whether the day will be fun for them, or a disaster. I'm the designated leader. If we go out for several hours, I grab the right equipment and supplies for all emergencies. (Actually, to be totally honest, it is their mom who pulls it all together!) We get tires pumped up, and gather the right clothes, food, and water for the journey. I must also be prepared for the pitfalls along the way: potholes, sunburn, thirst, windburn, scrapes, bruises, saddlesores, careening cars (therefore, helmets), and fatigue. The best biking equipment in the world is overshadowed by the smallest problem like a tiny leak and no repair kit, or a blazing sun and no sunscreen.

Leadership is like that. The good you do can be destroyed by the precautions you fail to take. No matter how skilled or gifted we are as leaders, one or two glaring blind spots can ruin our influence. A few bad habits can void the effectiveness of all our talents and accomplishments. The bottom line? An ounce of prevention is worth a pound of good leadership. Thus our need to take a look at some common leadership mistakes.

The privilege of leadership is a high calling . . . and adventure! Perhaps the significance of doing it right has been best summed up by George Bernard Shaw in *Man and Superman:*

> This is the true joy in life, the being used for a purpose recognized by yourself as a mighty one; the being a force of nature instead of a feverish selfish little clod of ailments and grievances complaining that the world will not devote itself to making you happy.
>
> I want to be thoroughly used up when I die, for the harder I work the more I live. I rejoice in life for its own sake. Life is no "brief candle" to me. It is a sort of splendid torch which I have got hold of for the moment, and I want to make it burn as brightly as possible before handing it on to future generations (Shaw, 1972:84).

$$\boxed{1}$$

# The Top-down Attitude
## *The Number-one Leadership Hang-up*

▶ The top-down attitude comes
naturally to most people.

▶ Servant leadership is much more rare.

▶ Effective leaders see themselves at
the bottom of an inverted pyramid.

I intended to save the best for last, like a top-ten count-down. But on second thought, I realize that this top-down-attitude problem is like the mother of all leadership hang-ups. If you have it you will spread it to everything your leadership hands touch. So it must come first as foundational to everything else I will observe about how not to lead.

At a conference of pastors and their wives in Northern California several months ago, I was speaking on the theme of top leadership mistakes. One man came up to me after a session and asked the obvious question: "Which

> "He that thinketh he leadeth . . . and hath no one following him . . . only taketh a walk."
> — Dr. John Maxwell

is the top of the top ten?" I believe that the number one leadership sin is that of top-down autocratic arrogance.

You would think people would have learned by now. Yet it still keeps cropping up, that age-old problem of domineering, autocratic, top-down leadership. Of all the sins of poor leadership, none is greater and none is still committed more often, generation after generation.

The top-down approach to leadership is based on the military model of barking orders to weak underlings. It goes something like this: "I'm in charge here, and the sooner you figure that out the better!"

Take, for example, this story related to me by one of my students when I was teaching a course on leadership:

My organization was looking for a new regional leader. They had somebody picked out. However, before finalizing it, they were going to meet with different individual leaders to receive feedback on the individual they had chosen. I gave them my serious concerns and observations. Even though they took the time to listen to us, they really didn't hear what we were saying. In the end, our input and feedback was rejected. And our predictions came to pass.

How did this whole situation make us feel? We concluded that the leaders at the top had already made up their minds regarding their choice, and that, almost as an afterthought, they had decided to talk to us "underlings" to try to get our rubber-stamp approval. It made me feel as if they didn't really want or need my input. If they would have listened to us, we would have been spared the pain, misunderstanding, and hurt when it became obvious to everyone that this individual was the wrong choice for leadership.

### Where "Top-down" Shows Up

- Abusive authority
- Deplorable delegation
- Lack of listening
- Dictatorship in decision-making
- Lack of letting go
- Egocentric manner

One blatantly irritating practice of some leaders who exercise a top-down style is the use of knowledge—or really the lack thereof—to keep people in line and in place.

Knowledge in an organization is power. A leader can use this power to dominate underlings by keeping them guessing and in the dark.

Dictators have long recognized that knowledge is their worst enemy. I grew up in the Deep South — in Alabama —

---

### Understanding Young Workers

With more and more younger workers on the scene, managers need to understand what turns them on and off.

**Turn-ons**

* Recognition and praise.
* Time spent with managers.
* Learning how what they're doing now is making them more marketable.
* Opportunities to learn new things.
* Fun at work — structured play, harmless practical jokes, cartoons, light competition, and surprises.
* Small, unexpected rewards for jobs well done.

**Turn-offs**

* Hearing about the past — especially yours.
* Inflexibility about time.
* Workaholism.
* Being watched and scrutinized.
* Feeling pressured to convert to traditionalist behavior.
* Disparaging comments about their generation's tastes and styles.
* Feeling disrespected.

— *Lawrence J. Bradford and Claire Raines,* Twenty-something, *1992.*

where the whites kept the blacks ignorant so that their knowledge could not become dangerous. I'll never forget the day our governor stood before the entrance to the University of Alabama to bar a young black girl from being our state's first black student at a "white" university. It was a sick and mistaken attitude of arrogance that, fortunately for us all, soon crumbled.

If people are kept in the darkness of ignorance, they are less likely to revolt against a ruthless ruler. For that reason, communist border guards for years were ordered to confiscate current magazines and newspapers from Western tourists. In the years that I traveled in Eastern Europe, the border guards always asked us if we had three categories of "contraband": weapons, books and magazines, and Bibles. They knew that if the truth got into the hands of the citizens, the task of maintaining tyranny would become more difficult.

*The Royal Bank Letter,* a Canadian publication, made this observation:

> A prophetic expert on the subject of tyranny through ignorance, Adolph Hitler, wrote in *Mein Kampf* that propaganda, to be effective, must operate on the level of the "most stupid" members of society. Hitler, who loathed universal education, knew that ignorance goes hand-in-hand with gullibility. He realized that he could best "work his wicked will," as Winston Churchill put it, when his audience was kept in the dark.

Top-down leadership can become like a chain reaction. The boss barks orders to the employee. The employee goes home and barks orders at his spouse. The spouse barks orders at the children. The children kick the dog, and the dog chases the neighborhood cat! It comes so natural to most of us to be autocratic but it also happens to be a great leadership mistake.

Why do a lot of people fall into the trap of top-down

leadership attitudes? For at least five reasons:

**1. It's traditional.** Historically, autocratic, top-down leadership has been the most commonly practiced method.
**2. It's the most common.** Even though much has been written about alternative forms of leadership, top-down leadership is still the most common kind.
**3. It's the easiest.** It is much easier to simply tell people what to do than to attempt other, much more effective, leadership styles.
**4. It comes natural.** For some reason, the natural self prefers to domineer others, and to try to amass power that can be held over other people. Leadership by nature seems to mean one person "over" another.
**5. It reflects the depravity of man.** Satan began the problem when he wanted to get out from under submission to God the Father. So he rebelled and led his own band of rebels to bring rebellion to the world.

### Contrasting Two Approaches

Much has been said in recent years about new styles of leadership that oppose top-down, autocratic leadership. They come with new labels like participatory management, the "flat" organizational style, democratic leadership, or the model which I prefer to call servant leadership. Servant leadership embraces all these new models, and it is built on Christ's model of leadership.

A source book on this different kind of leadership is *Servant Leadership*, by Robert K. Greenleaf. The book is subtitled, "A Journey into the Nature of Legitimate Power and Greatness." He defines the whole process of servant leadership in these terms:

A new moral principle is emerging which holds that the only authority deserving one's allegiance is that which is freely and knowingly granted by the led to the leader in response to, and in proportion to, the clearly evident servant stature of the leader. Those who choose to follow this principle will not casually accept the authority of existing institutions. Rather, they will freely respond only to individuals who are chosen as leaders because they are proven and trusted as servants (Greenleaf, 1977:9–10).

More than thirty years ago a landmark book began the revolution away from dictatorial leadership. In 1960, Douglas McGregor published the *Human Side of Enterprise,* in which he outlined what became known as "Theory X versus Theory Y" leadership style. Basically, McGregor believed that people really did want to do their best work in organizations, and if properly integrated into ownership of the goals of the organization, they would control themselves and do their best.

The book must be seen in the context of the times in which it was written. In the 1950s and 1960s, there was a backlash against strong, centralized, authoritarian leadership styles. McGregor rode the wave of that changing attitude in our society and developed his Theory Y leadership model. It was based on respect for individual workers, and gave them much more participation in their supervision and direction, with less rigid direction and control in the hands of their supervisors.

McGregor began what I see as the healthy trend toward servant leadership in the business world, and helped move organizations toward a biblical model of leadership. His early theories are at the foundation of a lot of popular management philosophy in the 1990s. I have summarized his "Theory X versus Theory Y" approach in the following chart. As you note the two columns, it is easy to see that Theory X is the top-down leadership attitude. It never ceases to amaze me that thirty years of awareness of Theory Y and other leadership alternatives has not penetrated the craniums of some bull-headed leaders.

Based on a new look at human nature, and drawing heavily from motivational theory, Theory Y says that work can be enjoyable and workers can do their best when trusted to motivate themselves in their work. Workers *should be allowed to self-direct and self-control their tasks* out of the respect and trust coming from management.

Theory X focuses on tactics of direction and control through the exercise of authority. Theory Y, on the other

| Theory X | Theory Y |
|---|---|
| 1. Work is inherently distasteful to most people. | 1. Work is as natural as play, if conditions are favorable. |
| 2. Most people are not ambitious, have little desire for responsibility, and prefer to be directed. | 2. Self-control is often indispensable in achieving organizational goals. |
| 3. Most people have little capacity for creativity in solving organizational problems. | 3. The capacity for creativity in solving organizational problems is widely distributed in the population. |
| 4. Motivation occurs only at the physiological and safety levels. | 4. Motivation occurs at the social, esteem, and self-actualization levels, as well as physiological and security levels. |
| 5. Most people must be closely controlled and often coerced to achieve organizational goals. | 5. People can be self-directed and creative at work if properly motivated. |

—*Hersey and Blanchard, 1982:49*

hand, focuses on the nature of human relationships — the integration of personal goals with the success of the enterprise.

## Superior or Servant?

What is servant leadership "in the nitty-gritty"? Let me give you a couple of examples from my own recent experience.

As with most mornings at the office, this one started quite typically for me. I had many items on my own agenda: read important papers, write important letters, call several important meetings, make numerous important decisions, and answer only the important phone calls. The idea was that I would sit behind my big desk and others would come to me with their requests.

Wrong! Within an hour I found myself in the basement of our office, helping clear out shelves and throwing away trash. I was helping my facilities manager prepare a new area for a library that we would build — because of a directive I had initiated. A servant leader must be willing to get "down and dirty" with his troops in the implementation of his objectives.

The top-down attitude would be characterized by the person who believes that everyone should serve them, as opposed to them serving the others in the institution. In reality, it seems to me that everyone in our organization rests on my shoulders and I am at the bottom of an inverted pyramid. I spend countless hours helping others be effective by providing them the facts, the energy, the resources, the networks, the information, or whatever else they need to do an effective job. Most of my day is spent laying aside my own priorities to help others fulfill theirs. Sometimes that will require hours of nitty-gritty work alongside those workers to help them get their jobs done. Recently I spent half an hour searching through a hard disk for a lost file that a secretary desperately needed. Since I knew the most about how to find the files within that computer, I deemed it important to take my time to look for it. (I did find it, by the way, to everyone's great relief!)

Servant leadership requires us to sit and weep with those who weep within our organizations. It requires getting down and dirty when hard work has to be done. There is nothing in my organization that anyone does that I should not be willing to do myself if it promotes the good of us all.

People follow leaders for many reasons. The chart on page 34 shows the "five levels of leadership" as described by Dr. John Maxwell. He points out clearly that the most effective and authentic type of leadership is that which is based on one's personhood — respect for the leader. People follow you because of who you are and what you represent.

## The One Who Showed Us the Way

When it comes to servant leadership there is no better model than that of Jesus Christ. On the night He was betrayed, Jesus showed His followers just how much He loved them. We read in John chapter 13, verse 1, that He "knew that the time had come for Him to leave this world and go to the Father. Having loved His own who were in the world, He now showed them the full extent of His love." At that point Jesus begins to give His final and ultimate demonstration of servant leadership: He washes the disciples' feet!

The first thing I notice in this passage is Jesus' all-encompassing power and authority. The foundation for His servanthood was a true realization of His power, position, and prestige. He was God Himself in the flesh, and had every right to be a dictator. In fact, He is the one and only man who has ever walked on the face of the earth who has had the right to be an absolute autocrat.

Having this foundation, Jesus demonstrated servant leadership by taking off His robe, picking up a towel, and washing His disciples' feet. If I had been there that night, I would have been embarrassed beyond words the moment I saw Him pick up the towel and begin to wash the first set of feet. I would have been embarrassed and humiliated because I had not been willing to lower myself to the dirty task of foot-washing. Yet Jesus demonstrated that He who was to be greatest among His followers would be servant of all.

---

### No Desire to Lead

A true and safe leader is likely to be one who has no desire to lead, but is forced into a position of leadership by the inward pressure of the Holy Spirit and the press of the external situation. Such were Moses and David and the Old Testament prophets. I think there was hardly a great leader from Paul to the present day but that was drafted by the Holy Spirit for the task, and commissioned by the Lord of the Church to fill a position he had little heart for. I believe it might be accepted as a fairly reliable rule of thumb that the man who is ambitious to lead is disqualified as a leader. The true leader will have no desire to lord it over God's heritage, but will be humble, gentle, self-sacrificing and altogether as ready to follow as to lead, when the Spirit makes it clear that a wiser and more gifted man than himself has appeared.

*—A.W. Tozer*

---

The explanation of His servant leadership comes at the end of the passage, when Jesus says, "I have set you an example that you should do as I have done for you. I tell you the truth, no servant is greater than his master, nor is a messenger greater than the one who sent him. Now that you know these things, you will be blessed if you do them" (vv. 15-17).

Another passage of Scripture that speaks eloquently about servant leadership is 1 Peter 5:1-7:

To the elders among you, I appeal as a fellow elder, a witness of Christ's sufferings and one who also will share in the glory to be revealed: Be shepherds of God's flock that is under your care, serving as overseers—not because you must, but because you are willing, as God wants you to be; not greedy for money, but eager to serve; *not lording it over those entrusted to you,* but being examples to the flock. And when the Chief Shepherd appears, you will receive the crown of glory that will never fade away.

Young men, in the same way be submissive to those who are older. *Clothe yourselves with humility toward one another,* because, God opposes the proud but gives grace to the humble. Humble yourselves, therefore, under God's mighty hand, that He may lift you up in due time. Cast all your anxiety on Him because He cares for you (emphasis mine).

## POWERPOINTS

What are the alternatives to the top-down attitude hang-up? In terms of leadership style, I would summarize them as:

**1. Participatory management.** Give the group of workers or members the privilege of input before you move on a course of action. This is messier and more time-consuming, but it motivates and inspires people.

**2. Facilitator style.** See your role as that of a facilitator who makes it possible for those who work for you to be successful. You are there to empower others for effective work.

**3. Democratic leadership.** Build a leadership team with a democratic process that enables the group to have a vital role in the nature and direction of their organization.

**4. Flat organizational characteristics.** View yourself as side-by-side or leading the charge, but not as being on the top of a giant pyramid. More on this in chapter 5.

**5. Servant leadership.** If He who is Lord of lords and King of kings was a servant of all, how can I, in my right mind, think that I should be served by those I lead?

---

"Christ Jesus . . . made himself nothing.
He made himself nothing, emptied himself—the great *kenosis.* He made himself no reputation, no image."

I can recall my father shaking his head and repeating over and over to himself, "If I only knew what this meant. There is something powerful here. If I only understood it." Maybe that is why this Scripture has glued itself to my mind and equally disturbs me. Reputation is so important to me. I want to be seen with the right people, remembered in the right light, advertised with my name spelled right, live in the right neighborhood, drive the right kind of car, wear the right kind of clothing. But Jesus made himself of no reputation!

—*Gayle D. Erwin,* The Jesus Style, *1988*

---

How then can I lead without the arrogance of a top-down attitude? If my desire is to be a servant leader as I maintain my responsibilities of authority in the organization, what are my guiding principles? Try these powerpoints on for size:

- ☑ Not abusive authority, but servant of all (John 13).
- ☑ Not deplorable delegation, but give people room and freedom to be themselves.
- ☑ Not lack of listening, but focus on the needs of others (Phil. 2).
- ☑ Not dictatorship, but partners in the process.
- ☑ Not holding on, but letting go with affirmation.
- ☑ Not egocentric, but empowering others.

The legend on page 35 illustrates the significance of quiet servant leadership:

## The Five Levels of Leadership
"Why People Follow Other People"

**5. POSITION (Title) "Rights"**

☑ **People follow because they have to.**

Your influence will not extend beyond the lines of your job description. The longer you stay here, the higher the turnover and lower the morale. People begin to limit you; to put fences around you. You can't stay here more than two years.

**4. PERMISSION "Relationships"**

☑ **People follow because they want to.**

People will follow you beyond your stated authority. This level allows work to be fun. Caution: staying too long on this level without rising will cause highly motivated people to become restless.

**3. PRODUCTION "Results"**

☑ **People follow because of what you have done for the organization.**

This is where success is sensed by most people. They like you and what you are doing. Problems are fixed with very little effort because of momentum. (Don't let the momentum stop!)

**2. PEOPLE DEVELOPMENT "Reproduction"**

☑ **People follow because of what you have done for them personally.**

This is where long range growth occurs. Your commitment to developing leaders will insure ongoing growth to the organization and to people. Do whatever you can to achieve and stay on this level.

**1. PERSONHOOD "Respect"**

☑ **People follow you because of who you are and what you represent.**

This step is reserved for leaders who have spent years growing people and organizations. Few make it. Those who do are bigger than life!

—*Dr. John Maxwell,* Developing the Leader within You, *1993*

As construction began on a magnificent cathedral, an angel came and promised a large reward to the person who made the most important contribution to the finished sanctuary. As the building went up, people speculated about who would win the prize. The *architect?* The *contractor?* The *woodcutter?* The *artisans* skilled in gold, iron, brass, and glass? Perhaps the *carpenter* assigned to the detailed grillwork near the altar? Because each workman did his best, the complete church was a masterpiece. But when the moment came to announce the winner of the reward, everyone was surprised. It was given to an old, poorly dressed peasant woman. What had she done? Every day she had faithfully carried hay to the ox that pulled the marble for the stonecutter.

# Putting Paperwork
# before Peoplework
## *Confessions of an*
## *Obsessive-compulsive*

▶ The greater the leadership role,
  the less time there seems to be for people.

▶ The greater the leadership role,
  the more important peoplework is.

▶ People are opportunities, not interruptions.

▶ Only through association is there transformation.

N ot long ago Pacific Bell in Southern California was forced to add another area code in Los Angeles. One PR firm offered this explanation:

All the car phones called the answering machines,
which dialed into voice mail,
then transmitted by modem to beep the pagers
that forwarded the calls via E-mail to fax the
message heard 'round L.A.:
"Let's do lunch."

All of us task-oriented obsessive-compulsives must learn to slow down and let people into our lives. It may be popular in the '90s to be a fast-tracker with a full Daytimer, but we will only impact people spiritually and permanently by that one-on-one contact that can't be substituted. In this age of telecommunications and teleconnecting, there is still no substitute for quiet, prolonged exposure of one soul to another.

I'm German, and therefore tend to be task-oriented. Since I find myself in roles of leadership, I often think about how my Germanness affects my leadership. Is it an unfair generalization to say that Germans are all task-oriented? Well, think about any Germans you know. Do they tend to be perfectionists, accomplishers of great deeds, workaholics who rarely relax, and generally rigid in relationships? Probably. Sure, there are exceptions, but not among the many Germans I've known!

My beautiful, relationally oriented wife is always crying out to me, "Hans, stop! Can't you just sit down for an hour and do nothing? Could we just talk?" That is extremely hard for me to do . . . to do "nothing." I guess that, deep down in my task-oriented nature, I see talking as not really accomplishing all that much, so I tend toward being an impatient conversationalist — that is, unless I am in a deep discussion that is driving me toward the accomplishment of another task. Or, unless I am in a situation where I cannot immediately get to my work and therefore have some "down time." Even when we go camping I tend to spend my time tinkering with the equipment instead of just vegetating — which I think someone told me was the actual goal of this exercise.

---

### Signs of a Paper-pusher

- "People bother me — they are interruptions."
- "I prefer to be alone — to get my work done."
- "Ministry would be great — except for the people!"
- Out of touch with the networks and currents in the workplace.
- Tends to run over people — insensitive
- Listens poorly — if at all
- Impatient — tend to say, "Out with it!"
- Alone, aloof, and lonely
- Self-worth based on accomplishment

---

I like to use this cultural heritage bent as an illustration to focus on a certain type of behavior. In the area of leadership, it would be called a task-oriented style of leadership.

### People: Opportunities or Interruptions?

There is a simple test I have devised to discover whether a person is task-oriented or the opposite, people-oriented. It's very unscientific, but completely reliable! When someone walks into your office, or wherever you happen to work, and interrupts your task at hand for the sake of conversation, how do you react? Do you view that person as an interruption or an opportunity? Does your face brighten as your people antenna powers up, or do you grimace inside at this "interruption"? If you relax and converse until the chat has natural closure, you're obviously a people person. But if you press to squirm your way out of the conversation with a bombardment of verbal and nonverbal clues, then you are one of us: the dreaded obsessive-compulsives.

If a person's gut-level instinct in that situation is to get back to the task at hand

> **Why do we put paperwork before peoplework?**
>
> - Seen results take priority over the unseen relationship.
> - Taskwork pushes aside "idle" talk.
> - The material world predominates over the immaterial world.
> - We feel we are judged by what we *do,* not who we *are.*
> - Obsessive-compulsive behavior.
> - Relationships don't fit our "deadlines" mentality.

at any cost, it is safe to assume that he or she is task-oriented. If, on the other hand, that interruption is not seen as one, and delightful, calm conversation ensues, then the interrupted person is probably people-oriented.

Nissan Motors used to have an ad slogan that declared, "We Are Driven." Well, task-oriented people are driven. I am so driven that my computer is a notebook I can take with me everywhere I go, so that I don't miss a chance to "task" in a spare moment. (I love that word so much I have made it a verb!)

> "A few years ago I met an old professor at the University
> of Notre Dame. Looking back on his long life of teaching,
> he said with a funny twinkle in his eyes: 'I have always
> been complaining that my work was constantly inter-
> rupted, until I slowly discovered that my interruptions
> were my work.'
>
> "This is the great conversion in life: to recognize and
> believe that the many unexpected events are not just dis-
> turbing interruptions of our projects, but the way in
> which God molds our hearts and prepares us for his
> return. . . . "
>
> *—Henri J. Nouwen,* Out of Solitude, *1974*

Psychologists and psychiatrists call this type of personality
*obsessive-compulsive.* For some reason, the ranks of professional Christian workers—especially leaders—are flooded
with the likes of these driven people. It is almost *necessary*
to be a workaholic to make it as a Christian leader. Unfortunately, many leaders are poor listeners because of this very
problem. And it seems that the cumulative effect of all these
obsessive-compulsive leaders takes a toll on the character and
spirit of the body of Christ today. We have all witnessed with
sadness the epidemic of Christian leaders crashing and burn-
ing in recent years. Do our organizations require too much of
us? Are we all destined for obsessive-compulsive burnout?

I have wondered more and more lately if all this "accomplishment" is really accomplishing all that much? If you're
highly motivated like I am, you love to have hundreds of
irons in the fire. You also just might be missing out on the
adventure of a lifetime that I am rediscovering—people!

### The Tension of Paperwork versus Peoplework
Before I learned better—and I am still learning—my task-
oriented style of leadership got me into big trouble as a
leader—into serious conflict with my coworkers. The place,
the organization, and the individuals are not important, be-

cause the scenario repeated itself constantly in many ways and in many places. Basically, I ran into a conflict of *role expectations*. One of the greatest sources of conflict between followers and their leaders has to do with this issue of role expectations. The role we see ourselves filling is expressed through our leadership style. It is the "dressing" of our job, how we appear to others. Sometimes, any good we are doing in leadership is totally obscured by a style that alienates our followers. That is what happened to me.

The group I was responsible to lead had absolutely no criticism of the way I performed my tasks. In fact, they would all agree that I produced perfection to a fault. I never failed in doing my job. But I did fail in the "being" aspect. The problem was that they wanted my *attention,* and I was always too busy to give it to them. I fulfilled my organizational duties, but neglected those intangible duties of "people work"—just being with people and showing that I care. I viewed my role as a leader primarily as taking care of all of the tasks and paperwork of my job. I was trying to serve my followers by taking care of all of their needs logistically. I solved many of their problems and carried the load of the organizational burden so that they could be free for their work.

But I failed in one great regard—the human element, that subjective, person-to-person contact so essential in ministry. Their conclusion: I didn't care about them. And all this time I thought

> ## The Maestro and People
>
> My intention always has been to arrive at human contact without enforcing authority. A musician, after all, is not a military officer. What matters most is human contact. The great mystery of music making *requires real friendship among those who work together.* Every member of the orchestra knows I am with him and her in my heart.
>
> —*Carlo Maria Giulini,*
> *Conductor,*
> *Los Angeles Philharmonic,*
> *quoted in Bennis and Nanus,*
> *Leaders, 1985*

that I was doing them a favor by accomplishing all those tasks for their benefit! It is like the father who works hard all his life to buy his children everything, then wakes up one day to hear them tell him, "You don't care about me." Does he? Of course! Did I care about the people I worked with? Of course! But I lost the opportunity to lead that group because my style got me into deep trouble. And it got me thinking about my need for a personal leadership style check-up.

## Task-oriented Leadership

Many if not most Christian leaders in our country today tend toward being task-oriented. Even if it is not their nature or personality, it seems that the job of the modern-day executive leader demands it. We evaluate people by their accomplishments. Task-oriented people are the ones who get put in charge in the first place. They rise to the top of organizations by virtue of the large volume of tasks that they have been able to shove out the door. And the information revolution creates an ever-growing pile of paperwork that the leader must somehow cope with and control.

Some people tend to be *task-oriented* and some tend to be *people-oriented*. The problem is, we have subtly made task-orientation more desirable in our leader selec-

> **People will never care how much you know until they know how much you care.**

tion process. But without a healthy emphasis on people, we're actually accomplishing nothing. Leadership is basically a people business. Experts confirm that the most effective leaders spend most of their time being with people and solving people problems. The leadership surveys of Warren Bennis and Burt Nanus spell it out in black and white: "What we have found is that the higher the rank, the more interpersonal and human the undertaking. Our top executives spend roughly 90 percent of their time concerned with the messiness of people problems" (Bennis & Nanus, 1985:56).

### The Problem of Mounting Paperwork

We live in an age of ever-increasing complexity. Organizations always evolve into more complex bureaucracies rather than into leaner, more streamlined movements. In the information technology explosion, the Christian leader is evermore bombarded with an increasing barrage of paperwork. Computers have added to the proliferation of things to write and things to read. Desktop publishing has given everyone a license to publish anything. So how can the busy leader cope? Who is to know what to read anymore? How can anyone even see the people through the piles of paper? These problems alone seem to demand a task-oriented leadership style.

Then there is the problem of the kind of people attracted into the ministry and selected for leadership. While I was in graduate school at Dallas Seminary, Dr. Paul Meier of Minirth and Meier Clinics was my professor for Christian Psychology and Personality Development. He told us that psychological testing of all incoming applicants into our school showed that the vast majority of entering seminary freshmen were of the obsessive-compulsive personality types. Why were they the ones applying? And why were they the ones accepted into the school? Because they managed to fill out the best application, with the most accomplishments? Are our graduate school applicants today chosen according to who they are, or according to what they have done?

And what comes out the other end, when the seminarian graduates after three or four years? Are our seminaries producing largely task-oriented leaders? *How much training and emphasis do our seminaries give in people skills?* When I finished seminary, I felt that I knew how to begin to tackle the *tasks* of ministry. In fact, I was quite confident in the skills I had picked up in those four intense years. But soon after arriving at my first church, I was shocked to learn how weak I was in peoplework training. Someone has joked, "I love the ministry; it's the people I can't stand!"

In this first ministry experience, I soon found myself scrambling to learn how to relate to boards, committees, chairpersons, families, counselees—and people everywhere! It was a frustrating job sorting out the role of pastor: shepherd to the needs of the flock (people) versus administrator of this large organization (production and paperwork). I felt that I had received next to no training in seminary in the fine art of nitty-gritty peoplework.

Paperwork is getting out of hand, and many people in leadership try in their obsessive-compulsive ways to manage this increasingly unmanageable task. Or they ignore the flow and are accused of dropping the ball with poor leadership skills. Or, more common than not, they crash and burn—not a lovely sight. Meanwhile, the *people* in the body of Christ continue to hurt, to cry out for the attention of professionals who have little time to touch their wounds.

### Whatever Happened to Peoplework?

Not long ago I decided to read through the Gospels in the New Testament, to underline all the leadership principles I could find demonstrated by the life of Jesus. I made an amazing discovery: *Jesus spent more time touching people and talking to them than in any other action.* Jesus was not primarily task-oriented, even though He knew He had only three years to train twelve men to carry on the movement that would change the world!

Touching wounds amid the unbearable pressure to perform tasks—that was the model of our Lord Jesus Christ. If you stay alert to the two words *crowd* and *multitude* in the Gospels, you will be amazed to see how often

### The Shepherd's Touch

- He knew them:
  John 10:14-15
- He touched them:
  Luke 4:40
- He healed them:
  Matthew 15:30
- He affected them:
  Luke 6:40
- He mentored them:
  John 13:15-17

our Lord was smothered by the press of the crowds. At the end of one of His busiest days it is recorded that,

> When the sun was setting, the people brought to Jesus all who had various kinds of sickness, and laying His hands on each one, He healed them (Luke 4:40).

What is the ministry all about? People, or production? Obviously, much of the paperwork and production is aimed at helping people. But too often there is little time or energy left for people at the end of the exhausting efforts of accomplishing those tasks.

Whether we like to admit it or not, paperwork, deadlines, and crowded Daytimers often preoccupy us and create a barrier between us and the opportunity for touching people's lives in a transforming way.

### Influencing People: A Transformational Issue

As I suggested at the outset, the heart of leadership is influencing others. For the Christian leader, it is influencing God's people to move toward God's purposes. But isn't one of God's first and greatest purposes the transformation of character? The Apostle Paul, greatest accomplisher of tasks in the early church era, had as his driving passion the transformation of peoples' lives:

> We proclaim Him, admonishing and teaching everyone with all wisdom, *so that we may present everyone perfect in Christ.* To this end I labor, struggling with all His energy which so powerfully works in me (Col. 1:28-29, emphasis mine).

Every person who aspires to be used by God in His service must have as a prime objective the same passion: to see people's lives changed into Christ's likeness. For the Christian leader, his or her greatest impact will be lives changed through personal influence on followers.

### People Change People by Direct Contact

I was reminded of the battle to build relationships late one night at Mount Hermon, in the coastal mountains of northern California. At the time I was in my doctoral sabbatical program studying with a favorite professor, Bobby Clinton, in Southern California. Even though I had come to his school to "sit at his feet," over the first six months we had not managed to have even half an hour together to get to know each other personally. Our calendars just couldn't connect on a time. As chance would have it, we both ended up at Mount Hermon for a couple of days, with that rare commodity known as dead time. We decided to room together, and we stayed up past midnight one night, finally taking the time to begin the process of real relationship-building.

I learned more of value about Bobby Clinton in those three hours that night than in all the dozens of hours of classroom lectures and casual contact on campus.

How are people changed? How is it that we can influence others to be more Christlike? The clearest way to answer that is to ask a simple question: As you look back over your past, what has had the greatest impact on you, personally, in your growth as a leader or as a person? Has it been books, lectures, or tapes? Has it been sermons or church services? Has it been classroom experiences? Every survey I have ever heard about on this question comes back with one resounding answer: A person, or a number of key people with whom we have had real-life personal contact, have been the primary change agents in our lives. It may have been in the church, at a seminar or retreat, or in school. But it is always direct contact with a person that has the most powerful impact on our lives. Sure, we are influenced by many factors in small ways and at a distance, but the most profound changes in our lives come through the people who have *directly* influenced us.

The Scriptures are full of illustrations of the power of influence modeling—people changing people by personal

---

**Which Comes First, the Person or the Task?**

This is a question that has caused tension for centuries. Which is right depends on what you're doing.

If you're at a party, it's people first.

If you are fighting a fire, it's the task first.

Psalm 78:72 answers the question like a glittering diamond: "And David shepherded them with integrity of **heart**; with skillful **hands** he led them." The function of leaders is to feed and guide.

*—Lorne Sanny, for thirty years*
*General Director of the Navigators*

---

contact. It has been said that Christian growth is caught, not taught. We see this principle throughout the New Testament. Barnabas mentored Paul into a place of powerful usefulness. And Paul mentored Timothy to take over his own life's work. It is obvious that there was a deep personal relationship—not just casual contact at the office or in the classroom—between Paul and Timothy:

> You, however, know all about my teaching, my way of life, my purpose, faith, patience, love, endurance, persecutions, sufferings—what kinds of things happened to me in Antioch, Iconium and Lystra, the persecutions I endured (2 Tim. 3:10-11).

Paul had obviously made time for extensive people contact in the churches he had aggressively planted. For example, he writes to the Philippians:

> Whatever you have learned or received or heard from

me, or *seen in me* — put it into practice. And the God of peace will be with you (Phil. 4:9, emphasis mine).

Regardless of what orientation one has in leadership style — task or people — effective leaders make room for people. Leaving them out is a big, big leadership mistake.

If you are wired like I am to enjoy working alone and working on tasks, you must reorient yourself to people. People will only be influenced and changed as we allow them into our personal lives.

## Make Room for People

Thomas Watson, founder of IBM, built one of the most successful companies in history because he never allowed the organization to replace people as his number-one focus. During one meeting in the early days of IBM, a number of managers were reviewing customer problems with Mr. Watson. On the table were eight or ten piles of papers, identifying the sources of problems: manufacturing problems, engineering problems, and the like. After much discussion, Watson, a big man, walked slowly to the front of the room and, with a flash of his hand, swept the table clean and sent papers flying all over the room. He said, "There aren't any categories of problems here. There's just one problem: *Some of us aren't paying enough attention to our customers.*" He turned crisply on his heel and walked out, leaving twenty fellows wondering whether or not they still had jobs (Peters and Waterman, 1985:159).

It doesn't hurt to take a lesson from a successful company. In the ministry of leadership, people must take priority over paper and production. Yes, we may tend toward one style because of our personalities. But no, we are not to use that as an excuse to ignore and avoid people.

Isn't it funny that we have to remind ourselves that the goal of all ministry is people!

## *POWERPOINTS*

Bill Clinton won the election in November 1992 largely because people in America wanted change and because his handlers helped him focus. He focused on what people cared most about. In their war room, the then-governor's key aides put up a huge banner to remind them daily of their target: "It's the economy, stupid." I have to remind myself constantly that as a leader my banner must read, "IT'S THE PEOPLE, STUPID." If I neglect this advice, I am indeed the stupid one.

Someone has said that a man's best friend, aside from the dog, is the wastebasket. How often do I find myself lost in the paperwork and production work of ministry, and forget to stay connected to the people? My predecessor at CBFMS, Dr. Warren Webster, had a slogan on his desk which he lived out: "People Count." He was right, and he left me a hard act to follow.

---

### How to Push aside the Paper

- ☑ Love your wastebasket.
- ☑ Do lunches away from work.
- ☑ Take time off with your spouse, children, and friends.
- ☑ Plan get-a-ways with combinations of the above.
- ☑ Pray for people.
- ☑ Jog with your colleagues.
- ☑ Change locations to get out among people.
- ☑ Delegate more.
- ☑ Learn to "ransack" instead of reading everything.
- ☑ See people as priority one.
- ☑ MBWA, manage by wandering around.

---

We task-oriented compulsives are fanatics about the future. We live there. I am always planning and working for

### THREADS

Sometimes you just connect,
like that,
no big thing maybe
but something beyond the usual business stuff.
It comes and goes quickly
so you have to pay attention,
a change in the eyes
when you ask about the family,
a pain flickering behind the statistics
about a boy and a girl in school,
or about seeing them every other Sunday.
An older guy talks about his bride,
a little affectation after twenty-five years.
A hot-eyed achiever laughs before you want him to.
Someone tells about his wife's job
or why she quit working to stay home.
An old joker needs another laugh on the way
to retirement.
A woman says she spends a lot of her salary
on an au pair
and a good one is hard to find
but worth it because there's nothing more important
than the baby.
Listen.
In every office
you hear the threads
of love and joy and fear and guilt,
the cries for celebration and reassurance,
and somehow you know that connecting those threads
is what you are supposed to do,
and business takes care of itself.

*—James A. Autry,* Love and Profit, *1991:26*

goals out there in the distance. My preoccupation is chasing that shooting star, that next great task I want to accomplish. It is hard for me to sit still in the here-and-now, because I have so many irons in the fire for the greater day "out there." It is as if a giant magnet is always pulling my attention and energy into the future.

But every once in a while I stop and take time to look back. I ask myself, *Okay, Hans, if it were all over today, what do you have to show for yourself?* If I had no more time left to heap up more accomplishments, would I be satisfied with the works I could lay at the feet of Jesus? My answer is quite sobering.

The things I look back on and feel a lasting sense of accomplishment about always have to do with the people I have influenced—people who are different in a positive way, because their lives intersected mine at some point. In rare moments of my life, with not enough frequency, I have allowed others to come into my life and have laid aside my agenda for theirs.

When someone comes into my office or interrupts me on the phone, my gut reaction is to see it as an interruption. But God is showing me that I have to make room for people in my life. When all is said and done, the crowns of my achievements will not be the systems I managed, the things I wrote, the structures I built, but the people I personally, permanently influenced through direct contact.

## 3

# The Absence of Affirmation
## *What Could Be Better than a Pay Raise?*

▶ Everyone thrives on affirmation and praise.

▶ Leadership has as much to do with the "soft sciences" as with getting things done.

▶ We wildly underestimate the power of the tiniest personal touch of kindness.

▶ Learn to read the varying levels of affirmation your people need.

After thirty years of marriage, his wife was ready to finally throw in the towel. "I have had it, living with you," she moaned in disgust. "You never tell me you love me. It has been *years* since I have heard those three words come out of your mouth."

In a stoic, cool manner the husband replied, "Look, I told you I loved you when we got married—if I change my mind I'll let you know."

Organizational researchers have been telling us for years that affirmation motivates people much more than financial incentives, but we still don't get it. People thrive on praise. It does more to keep the people who work for you and with you fulfilled than fortune or fame could do.

How many bosses expect their associates to run on autopilot, as did the hardhearted husband? Do you work for someone who expects the impossible but never encourages you? If you do, I know you are having a hard time at your job. Do you have people who work for you whom you never encourage with a kind word of appreciation or a note of encouragement? Try it, and watch the reactions!

I find little resemblance between the people I work with and the Energizer Bunny. That pink bunny keeps showing up and going, and going, and going. Humans couldn't be more opposite to this. They need to have their emotional batteries charged often. I have seen in some quarters in my own organization an attitude that people are expected to work out of a sense of duty—so why bother with this thing called praise? Christian organizations are sometimes the worst, because there is the attitude that: "They are working for the Lord, and He will reward them for their labors." Some even argue that it builds up egos to give men praise, therefore it is unspiritual and is to be avoided at all cost.

I find that a pretty sad argument against lavishing your coworkers with affirmation and recognition for a job well done. Yes, I am working for that final pat on the back in the sky, "Well done, good and faithful servant." But I think God expects me to pat others on the back along the way.

Two incidents recently reconfirmed my conviction that everyone needs a good deal of encouragement. One has to do with Roller Blades, the other with home mortgages.

I finally gave in to my five-year-old. For months, he has wanted roller blades like his two older brothers, but we just didn't want to get into that danger for our "baby." After running out of excuses to delay the purchase, we went out the night before last and picked out a nice pair—kids' size 13—that should do him for a good year or so. After the purchase the six of us stopped off for a quick supper, during which Andrew could of course think of nothing but those blades. Though it was now dark, we promised him that he could take them for a spin when we got home.

Andrew stood there like a brand-new pony trying to stand for the first time. Wobbly and unsure of himself, he insisted (to my delight) on hanging onto me as I pulled him up and down the driveway. In fact my twelve-year-old, Mark, got into the act as Andrew hung between us, dragging his feet as they kept rolling out from under him.

Now it is two days later. Do you think Andrew is still hanging onto us for support? Not a chance. As a matter of fact I just glanced out the window and he was playing goalie in a street hockey game with the neighborhood crew. Andrew needed a great amount of support at the early end of a new learning experience, but soon developed his own "skate legs." Affirming those who work for us and with us follows the same principle. They need the most at the early stages of a new job or assignment. Which leads to the story of the home mortgage.

My wife and I had dinner out the other night with our neighbors Keith and Sandy. The four of us are becoming

> ### Compliments Dissolve
>
> "One of the commodities in life that most people can't get enough of is compliments. The ego is never so intact that one can't find a hole in which to plug a little praise. But, compliments by their very nature are highly biodegradable and tend to dissolve hours or days after we receive them — which is why we can always use another."
>
> — *Phyllis Theroux*

great friends. Between the two couples there are seven children under twelve, so you can imagine the break it is for us to go out for a quiet evening.

After much fear and second-guessing, two weeks ago Keith quit his job and leaped careers from salesman for heating and air-conditioning products to a white-collar desk job in the home mortgage business. "So how is it going, Keith?" I asked as we settled down in our booth for a quiet evening of conversation. "I feel worthless," was his reaction. "There is nothing that I do right the first time, because everything is new to me."

I told Keith that it reminded me of the trauma we went through moving to a foreign country a decade ago — a helpless feeling like a child starting life over from scratch. It seemed to Keith that there was nothing about this job that related to any of his past experience. In his former job, he was a top salesman with a great sense of personal pride in his abilities. Now he was starting life over at ground zero.

Then Keith gave the clincher that ties into this issue of

affirmation: "I lap up every little word of encouragement like a thirsty puppy. It's the only thing that keeps me going." The people who are working around Keith right now have no idea how much their pats on the back are keeping him going.

### Different Strokes

The different people who work with you and for you will require different doses and different kinds of affirmation. In

| The Affirmation Continuum | |
|---|---|
| **Desperados** | **Auto-pilots** |
| Little confidence | Self-reliant |
| Laps up affirmation | Skeptical of affirmation |
| "The more the better" | "Leave me alone" |
| Fragile | Tough as nails |

fact, I have come to see the varying need for affirmation as a sort of continuum, as shown in the chart above. Most people fall somewhere in the middle of this chart, though I find more in organizations that tend toward the desperados than I do the self-reliant islands who wish to be left alone. Here's how I would describe the various types of affirmation needs on this continuum:

*Desperados.* This is the group who can't get enough praise and good strokes. They are desperate for approbation. "Warm fuzzy" is their middle name. One person who works for me always seem to be on the brink of resigning, until we pull that person back from the brink with lavish praise and good strokes. Most new workers in a group need this kind of attention to assure them that they are going to be welcome and do a good job. In this early stage of his new job, Keith is definitely a desperado.

*Up-and-downers.* For a long time, Mary will go along just fine and work away with little need of attention. But then she will enter into an emotional valley. Personal problems? Trouble at home with the children? Who knows, but she will begin to show signs of needing more attention. A good leader learns to read the signs of upness and downness in the countenance of his people. One of my employees follows this pattern. If I have not interacted with him over long weeks on end, then I begin to get nervous that he may be down. So I seek him out and assure him that he is still just as valuable as he was the last time I pumped him up. Recently he was sick for a few days and missed work. I slipped a card under his door so that he would find it first

---

**Thank-you Notes:**
**A Tiny Human Touch Goes a Long Way**
**—Tom Peters**

We wildly underestimate the power of the tiniest personal touch. And of all personal touches, I find the short, handwritten "nice job" note to have the highest impact. (It even seems to beat a call—something about the tangibility.)

A former boss (who's gone on to a highly successful career) religiously took about 15 minutes (max) at the end of each day, at 5:30 P.M., 6:30 P.M., whenever, to jot a half-dozen paragraph-long notes to people who'd given him time during the day or who'd made a provocative remark at some meeting. I remember him saying that he was dumbfounded by the number of recipients who subsequently thanked him for thanking them.

—*Tom Peters,* The Business Journal, *"Management Excellence"*
*(September 9, 1991): 24*

---

when he got back to the office. In it I simply told him that he was missed. He is single and I think that makes it even more important, since he was home alone. I told him, "We missed you being around, not for what you do but for who you are as part of us." It meant a lot to him.

*"Normal" people.* Are there any? This is probably the vast majority of folks out there who work with us, and who grew up in normal, stable homes. On second thought, scratch that last statement. This is a dying breed! The more dysfunctional and tough a person's background, the more they are going to need your regular affirmation. My observation is that the younger generations need more nurturing than the more rugged Depression and World War II veterans.

*Auto-pilots.* These are the Energizer Bunnies. I have known a few people through the years who really didn't need any encouragement. They were so strong and so busy that any attempts at praising them would be nothing more than a pesky gnat flying around one's face. They would brush it off with a look of confusion. There are also a few people who view attempts at praise with great suspicion. What does he want from me? What is coming next? Is he buttering me up for the kill? These are skeptics and people who have probably had bad experiences with others taking advantage of them. With them, all we need do is cultivate kindness.

The concept of different strokes for different folks is not really new. In the New Testament the Apostle Paul uses it in 1 Thessalonians 5:14: "And we urge you, brothers, warn those who are idle, encourage the timid, help the weak, be patient with everyone."

This whole business of affirming those who work with us and for us is very simple: *Do it!* I keep boxes of various kinds of note cards and encouragement cards in my desk at the ready. Often I don't even bother with a separate card or letter when sending an affirmation. I just scribble a "Good job, well-done" on the margin of the paper and send it back. It communicates two things: One, I actually read it!

That, in and of itself, is a miracle in the kind of paper factory most of us work in. The second message it conveys is that I thought "he or she" did a good job. Those who work with me have learned that I don't automatically praise everything, for I have high standards and ideals. But there is always something good to be found, even in the people most difficult to work with.

Paul finishes that paragraph in 1 Thessalonians with this thought: "Make sure that nobody pays back wrong for wrong, [there's enough of that going around!] but always try to be kind to each other and to everyone else" (v. 15). I take this to heart in leadership. Every day I have as a goal to write at least three words of kindness to someone. I once read a poem that led me to develop the practice of not putting off praise if I think it is due someone:

> **Even if you have to correct someone, good supervisors are people who...**
>
> ♦ can step on your toes without messing up your shine.
> ♦ give people a shot in the arm without letting them feel the needle.

If you know that praise is due him
Now's the time to give it to him,
For he cannot read his tombstone when he's dead.

## POWERPOINTS

My twins reminded me the other day of another great lesson about affirming good work done by others. Affirmation doesn't last. It needs to be replenished after long dry periods. I travel a lot in my work so I often have to go through the unpleasant and downright gut-wrenching task of saying good-bye to all my kids before a trip. They are all still pretty young, the oldest being twelve, so they enjoy lots of hugs and kisses. The twins and I have this thing about "filling my cup" before I leave. If I'm going for five days I tell them as I'm saying good-bye, "Now I need my cup filled up with five days of hugs and kisses." They pounce on me as we roll on the floor as if in a sea of love, hugs, and kisses. They fill my cup. And in a different but similar way, I have to fill the cups of my co-workers as they run dry in the heat of their work.

One of my prime roles as a Christian leader is "to prepare God's people for works of service" (Eph. 4:12). I do that with a great deal of guidance and encouragement.

Bottom line? We encourage others by:

*Listening.* (James 1:19) Just because we are the leaders does not mean we are the prime talkers. The *L* in leader stands for listening.

> ### A Servant of Servants
>
> Let every day be a day of humility; condescend to all the weaknesses and infirmities of your fellow-creatures, cover their frailties, love their excellencies, encourage their virtues, relieve their wants, rejoice in their prosperities, compassionate their distress, receive their friendship, overlook their unkindness, forgive their malice, be a servant of servants, and condescend to do the lowliest offices of the lowest of mankind.
>
> *—From William Law,* A Serious Call to a Devout and Holy Life, *1967*

*Empathizing.* (Rom. 12:15) If others are happy, share their joy. If there is deep tragedy in their lives, stop everything and weep with them.

*Comforting.* (2 Cor. 1:3-4) We have gone through so much ourselves, and those experiences give us the richness as leaders to be able to comfort others when they go through the same pain.

*Carrying burdens.* (Gal. 6:2) This, after all, is the way we "fulfill the whole law of Christ."

### APPRECIATE THE EXTRA EFFORT

Former IBM vice president Buck Rodgers recalls the advice of a newspaper columnist, Dr. George Crane, whom he read as a teenager. Crane proposed the "Three-Compliments-a-Day Club."

He believed that if you "joined" this club, each day you would

- ☑ be motivated to look for good around you,
- ☑ make at least three people happy,
- ☑ feel good about yourself, and
- ☑ people would be drawn to you.

Rodgers says the idea seems pretty corny now, but it works. He suggests these embellishments:

**1. Get out of your office.** When someone does a good job, pay him or her a visit to say thanks. It'll make a bigger impact than a memo, a phone call, or an invitation to your office.

**2. Don't let good work be secret.** Ask managers under you to inform you of their subordinates' accomplishments. Employees are discouraged when their special efforts go unnoticed. They may feel it was wasted effort or, worse, think their boss is taking credit for their work. Rodgers always sends them a handwritten note of appreciation.

**3. Thank people publicly** in house organs, memos, at meetings and conferences. Formalize thanks whenever possible.

—*From Buck Rodgers,* Getting the Best Out of Yourself and Others, *1991*

**Encouraging.** (1 Thes. 5:11) Let people know often that they are doing a good job. Look for the good and point it out, and you'll see more and more good come from your colleagues. "Therefore encourage one another and build each other up, just as in fact you are doing."

# No Room for Mavericks?
## *They Bring Us the Future!*

▶ Mavericks can save us from the
slide toward institutionalism.

▶ Large organizations usually kill off
mavericks before they can take root.

▶ Mavericks make messes by their very nature —
the good messes institutions need.

▶ Learn to recognize truly useful mavericks.

Bill and Mary sat on the couch in my office and spilled their wounded emotions for over an hour. Here were two extremely gifted individuals who had helped grow their local church very aggressively through their entrepreneurial zeal. Of the entire team of five families of which they were a part, Bill and Mary have the greatest giftedness in the areas of growing, expanding, and building. Yet they are mavericks, and after just two years their team ejected them for their lack of "playing by the rules." They have become outcasts. The word that was relayed to me from the team was, "Don't send them back; we don't want them."

And what are those rules that Bill and Mary broke? As I pried for their offense, all I found was a lack of boring institutional conformity.

Like many others who live on the radical fringes of organizations, Bill and Mary have a hard time fitting into a rigid bureaucracy. They are mavericks and need freedom to fly.

Recently I led my senior staff through a discussion at one of our planning retreats on the topic of "making room for creative people." I challenged them with this question: Have we made it impossible for bright rising stars and maverick go-getters to live within our organization? When we become too preoccupied with policy, procedure, and the fine-tuning of conformity to organizational standards, in effect, we squeeze out some of our most gifted people.

Organizations have this nasty habit of becoming institutions. And institutions have this great tendency to fade into irrelevance. Movements become monuments. Inspiration becomes institution. The tragedy of this of-

> **"I'm looking for a lot of men with an infinite capacity for not knowing what can't be done."**
> — *Henry Ford*

ten-repeated story is that the older an organization gets, the less room there is for the entrepreneurially gifted. Mavericks are messy by nature, and calcified organizations chew them up and spit them out with their rigidity.

This is as true in the church as it is in the business world. There is a pattern that organizations follow, as they move from passion to paralysis, from the apostolic to the mechanistic. The pattern in fact seems to follow the very pattern of the human life cycle. There is every stage from birth to adolescence to the most productive adult years to, finally, death. Even organizations that don't die often look and act dead.

We can see the life cycles of organizations on the following chart. Let me briefly describe each stage. The time when mavericks are most crucial is during the entrepreneuring years of expansion in childhood and adolescence, and right after the crest during the graying years, when organizations need to be "born again."

***Birth.*** One or two individuals or families decide to try something new. They start a new business, plant a new church, or embark on some new enterprise that will create the new life of an organization.

***Infancy.*** The fragile new organization needs loads of tender loving care and constant feeding and pampering in

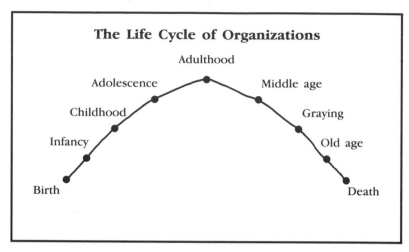

The Life Cycle of Organizations

these trying days of survival. And as new parents discover, there are many costs—and few paybacks beyond the joy of seeing the new life you have created.

***Childhood.*** The early, unsure days of floundering around, as the first steps are taken amid the bruises and bumps that come with childhood. Great learning is taking place.

***Adolescence.*** The identity crisis comes once the organization is up and running for sure. It comes somewhere between five and ten years out, when the original founding principles are questioned by the growing numbers of new members who were not there at the beginning. Great growth pains happen during this rite of passage to adulthood.

***Adulthood.*** The organization is now in its prime, fully staffed and functioning the way it was intended to from the beginning. These are great productive years, as things are going right and the goals are being accomplished in grand style.

***Middle age.*** As in human mid-life, things begin to slow down and some of the zest and zeal of the peak years is waning. Settling for limited objectives is very much part of the pattern here.

***The graying years.*** In these years institutionalization is taking place, or to put it more bluntly: fossilization. The preservation of the organization becomes the chief end, and new ideas are discouraged since they upset the established routines of the decades. "We've always done it that way" is the theme song of the graying years.

---

### Some Mavericks Who Made a Difference

+ **Martin Luther.** He nailed his convictions on a door, so the establishment couldn't miss it.

+ **The Apostle Paul.** What a turnaround! He went from being an outside destroyer to an inside promoter.

+ **William Carey.** When his superiors told him to sit down and shut up he ignored them, and became a mission hero.

+ **Lee Iacocca.** He came from outside to reinvent Chrysler from the top down.

+ **Chuck Colson.** From Nixon hatchet-man and the prison cell to modern-day prophetic voice for evangelical Christians.

+ **Martin Luther King.** He had a dream he was willing to die for, and he changed the very fabric of American life.

+ **Stephen Jobs.** Beginning in his garage with nothing but radical new ideas, he brought IBM to its knees.

---

**Old age.** If the organization is still around, it is just maintaining a bare existence — with a tiny market share of whatever it does. Nothing is happening, no one notices it and things are quiet in the orderly hallways and board rooms. Many churches in our land are in this condition, and can go on for years with the reserves of a few generous estates.

**Death.** Would that more organizations would take this bold move and vote themselves dissolved when they have fulfilled their usefulness. Every organization sooner or later must cease to have life, and we should allow each generation the privilege of creating its own vehicles to accomplish its ideals.

Birth, life, aging, and death: the natural order of creation. What do these life cycles have to do with *mavericks*? It should be obvious by now, that the older an organization, the less room for the truly creative. In the early years of a growing new organization, entrepreneurial vision and zeal is the very lifeblood that gets the group going. Whether a local church trying to attracting new members or a business going after a market share, it takes creative vision and go-getters to get things moving.

One of my students once asked me the obvious question about the "life-cycle" chart: "Can the decline down the other side of the curve be avoided, or is it inevitable?" I have grown more skeptical as the years have gone by, as I have viewed the comings and goings of organizations — what I call the ebb-and-flow of organizational life. There can be a rebirth, but it takes a strong dose of new blood — young, maverick blood — to arrest the slide down the far side of the life-cycle curve.

Most people who get to know me find that under the reserved German facade is a zealous maverick. So why would a fifty-year-old organization hire a young zealot like me to run things? I applaud the board of directors of our organization, not for selecting me, but for taking a gamble on putting a maverick in charge. We need it at this time in our life. We are in middle age, and many of the warning signs of the approaching graying years of institutional life are appearing in our midst. When the board of directors was interviewing me, they asked me my greatest fear for our organization—my gravest concern as we looked into the future. That was an easy question to answer for an organization like ours: "My greatest fear is that our best days were our past days. I loathe the thought that we should fade into irrelevance."

---

### The Eleven Commandments
### of Organizational Paralysis
### or . . .
### How to Put Mavericks in Their Place

- "That's impossible."
- "We don't do things that way around here. It's too radical a change for us."
- "We tried something like that before and it didn't work."
- "I wish it were that easy."
- "It's against policy to do it that way."
- "When you've been around a little longer, you'll understand."
- "Who gave you permission to change the rules?"
- "Let's get real, OK?"
- "How dare you suggest that what we are doing is wrong!"
- "If you had been in this field as long as I have, you would understand that what you are suggesting is absolutely absurd!"

---

One of the men who had a profound role of mentorship in my life in the 1980s was a fine gentleman and missionary statesman by the name of Arno Enns. Most people won't recognize his name, but the top ranks of our organization today is filled with men and women he mentored.

For ten years Arno was my boss and immediate supervisor. But he was more than that. After my own father died in 1984, he became like another dad for me. Now Arno is by his very nature cautious and process-oriented: Risk-taking is not natural for him. But he believed in me, and though I was a maverick in the organization, he cultivated me and harnessed that zeal. He gave me the opportunity to open our work in Eastern Europe in the early 1980s.

An incident in 1982 stands out as an example of how Arno was flexible enough to make room for me. We were living in Vienna, Austria and making forays into Eastern Europe as part of an underground leadership training ministry called Biblical Education by Extension. In the early months of 1982 I relayed a request back to him that I wanted to spend $3,900 for a personal computer. Remember, this was 1982. Most people had never heard of Stephen Jobs, and the IBM PC had yet to be released. I was going to purchase a Tandy Radio Shack TRS Model III personal computer for use in writing and for database chores. I was perhaps the first person in our overseas organization to make such a request. "Why would anyone need a *personal* computer?" was the general notion back then.

But Arno was different. He believed in me and thought that perhaps this was the way of the future. He listened to my arguments, and authorized the purchase as a sound one. It is partly because of that kind of visionary thinking that I have stuck with Arno and with the organization all these years. And now, at the helm myself, I have a passion to make room for the next generation of mavericks.

### Make Room for Mavericks

Webster defines a maverick as, "a pioneer an independent individual who does not go along with a group." Synonyms for maverick include nonconformist, heretic, dissident, dissenter, and separatist. If you think about it, Jesus was a maverick and was eventually destroyed by the institutional religious body—the Pharisees—He came to redeem. And you thought *you* had it tough getting your ideas through! The Scriptures are actually filled with men and women who were nonconformists—who didn't meet the norms of society. Moses was an outsider whom God chose to be an insider to bring renewal to His people. Joseph was left for dead by his brothers, they were so upset at his unusual ways. Peter was a maverick from the word go—seen most clearly when he told his Lord he would build three huts for Jesus, Moses, and Elijah during the Transfiguration. Jesus never cast him aside for his raw edge, but cultivated it and harnessed it. Then, of course, there was that great Pharisee of Pharisees, Paul, who like Martin Luther began in the bosom of the institution but soon was coloring outside the

---

*"The photograph is of no commercial value."*
Thomas Edison remarking on his own invention in 1880

*"There is no likelihood man can ever tap the power of the atom."*
Robert Millikan, Nobel prize winner in physics, 1920

*"It is an idle dream to imagine that automobiles will take the place of railways in the long-distance movement of passengers."*
American Road Congress, 1913

*"I think there is a world market for about five computers."*
Thomas Watson, chairman of IBM, 1943

*"There is no reason for any individual to have a computer in their home."*
Ken Olsen,
president of Digital Equipment Corporation, 1977

*—From Joel Barker,* Future Edge, *1992:89*

lines. Before you knew it he was sparking a fresh wind of renewal from heaven above.

A few years ago I read a fascinating book which traces the expansion of Christianity from the perspective of those who made it happen — *From Jerusalem to Irian Jaya,* by Ruth Tucker. It records the simple truth that the greatest strides in the advancement of the cause of Christ have come from the radical fringe, not the institutional core of the church. Likewise, the business and industrial world has been brought from one major era to another by the likes of strange inventors such as Thomas Edison and George Washington Carver. Chester Carlson who invented the Xerox process was laughed out of town before he finally patented his idea. The 3M Company encourages mavericks. The man who invented Post-it Notes did it on company time even though it was a personal project. The quartz movement watch was invented by a Swiss watchmaker; unfortunately his superiors rejected the idea, the Japanese and Americans patented it, and Switzerland went from an 85 percent global market share of watches to less than 15 percent.

I have this fear about mavericks in my own organization: I fear what they are going to want to do next — but not as much as what I fear if we lose them and they are not given the chance to do it for us. Most likely they will go ahead and do it for someone else!

### Breathing Room and Flexibility

One of the best ways to take the wind out of the sails of visionaries is to send their ideas to a committee. Here are some good definitions of committees:

An elephant is a horse designed by a committee.

A committee keeps minutes and wastes hours.

The best committee has three members — with two of them out of town.

A committee is made up of the unfit trying to lead the unwilling to do the unnecessary.

A committee is a collection of individuals who separately do nothing and together decide that nothing can be done.

It is a big mistake to stifle your brightest stars with the harnesses of endless committees, procedures, and paperwork. As I mentioned in chapter 1 on "the top-down" attitude, our understanding of leadership has been going through a paradigm revolution these last couple of decades. The "old way," exemplified by Henry Ford's production line, called for top managers to analyze the work that needed to be done, then devise detailed rules anyone could follow. Managers, divorced from the actual work, became bureaucrats while their frustrated subordinates tightened the bolts.

Those methods worked well during most of this century, but they won't help us much in the next. But many organizations and churches hang onto those attitudes and values of the past for one simple reason: The revolutionary process of change is agonizing. And working with mavericks involves risk-taking of major proportions.

I have been amazed at the transformation that has taken place in one of America's oldest and most stiffly bureaucratic institutions: General Electric. The maverick who is leading the charge is Jack Welch, who has brought about—admittedly with much pain—the "new way" at GE. Jack Welch's goal is to transcend the old concepts of management itself. Instead of seeking better ways to control workers, Welch says he aims to liberate them. As he explains, that goal is based on healthy self-interest:

The old organization was built on control, but the world has changed. The world is moving at such a pace that control has become a limitation. It slows you down. You've got to balance freedom with some control, but you've got to have more freedom than you ever dreamed of (Tichy and Sherman, 1993:20–21).

## POWERPOINTS

Let me make a plea with all of you who are in older institutions, to aim for flexible response amid policies and procedures. If you're on the board and in control, take some risk and bring some fresh young blood into the equation. You will be amazed what a few new faces can bring to a stagnant group of people. But give them room to succeed.

We must avoid the danger of the communists, who tried to make everyone equal, with no chance for true personal initiative. On my first trip to Russia in 1983, I was amazed when the tour guide pointed out that there was no unemployment in the land. I soon realized, as I studied the faces and learned the facts, that everyone had a job . . . but no one worked. The system killed all possibility for personal initiative and the results were—well, we all know what happened to that approach.

Don't allow your policies and procedures to stifle your brightest stars. Be flexible. Bend the rules, if you believe that someone needs more space.

Never be in bondage to your policy manual. Don't allow it to become the issue that drives away the most promising young Turks. Take risks and let people soar. Take this advice seriously: Goals should never arise out of corporate policy, company loyalty, or religious tradition alone.

Unless we're careful, we'll follow these four stages in the devolution of a fresh movement of God: (1) Men, (2) Movement, (3) Machines, (4) Monuments. The key to arresting or reversing this trend is to keep it a Holy Spirit-led and -inspired movement. How is that done? By allowing room for flexibility.

Not all troublemakers and malcontents are true mavericks. Some are just a pain to have around and don't do anyone much good. In the issue of working with mavericks and giving them room to flourish, there are three important areas to remember:

How to recognize legitimate mavericks who can bring you into the future:

- ☑ They care not just for their own ideas but for the goals of the organization.
- ☑ They are making a difference in their present position.
- ☑ They are willing to earn the right to be heard.
- ☑ Others are following their leadership—influence is taking place and it is producing good results.

How to encourage the true mavericks who can help you:

- ☑ Give them a long tether—they need space to soar.
- ☑ Put them in charge of something they can really own.
- ☑ Listen to their ideas and give them time to grow.
- ☑ Let them work on their own if they wish.
- ☑ Leave them alone and give them time to blossom.

How to stifle the mavericks in your midst:

- ☑ Have as many layers of management as possible for decisions to have to travel through.
- ☑ Keep looking over their shoulders.
- ☑ Make your policy manual as thick as possible.
- ☑ Control all important decisions at the top.
- ☑ Send everything possible to committees for deliberation.
- ☑ Always make them wait months for decisions that affect them. Put them on a team full of small-thinking bureaucrats.

And finally, a letter that came across my desk that might interest you.

The Rev. Paul, Apostle
Independent Missionary
Corinth, Greece

Dear Mr. Paul:

We recently received an application from you for service under our board. We have made an exhaustive
survey of your case and, frankly, we are surprised that
you have been able to "pass" as a bona-fide
missionary.

1. In the first place we are told that you are afflicted
with severe eye trouble which is almost certain to be
an insuperable handicap to any effective ministry. We
normally require 20-20 vision.

2. Secondly, we take a dim view of a full-time missionary doing part-time secular work, but we hear that
you are making tents on the side. You admitted in a
letter to the church at Philippi that they are the only
group supporting you. We wonder why this is.

3. Further, is it true that you have a jail record?
Certain brethren report that you did two years' time at
Caesarea and were also imprisoned in Rome.

4. Moreover, it is reported from Ephesus that you
made so much trouble for the businessmen there that
they refer to you as "the man who turned the world
upside down." We feel such sensationalism has no
place in missions. We also deplore the "over-the-wall-
in-a-basket" episode at Damascus.

5. In one of your letters you refer to yourself as
"Paul the Aged." Our new pension policies do not
anticipate a surplus of elderly recipients.

6. Your ministry has been far too flighty to be successful. First Asia Minor, then Macedonia, then Greece,
then Italy, and now you are talking about a wild-goose
chase into Spain. Concentration is more important
than dissipation of one's powers.

7. Finally, Dr. Luke the physician reports that you are a thin little man, rather bald, frequently sick, and always so agitated over your churches that you sleep very poorly. He indicates that you pad around the house praying half the night. *Our* ideal for all applicants is a healthy mind in a robust body. We believe that a good night's sleep will give you zest and zip so that you wake up full of zing.

We regret to inform you, Brother Paul, but in all our experience we have never met a candidate so opposite to the requirements of our mission board. If we should accept you we would be breaking every principle of current missionary practice.

Most sincerely,
J. Flavius Fluffyhead
Secretary, Foreign Mission Board

(Adapted Source Unknown)

# Dictatorship in Decision-making
## *Getting beyond, "I Know All the Answers"*

▶ Dictators deny the value of individuals.

▶ The major players in an organization are like its stockholders. They should have a say in its direction.

▶ The one who does the job should decide how it is done.

▶ "Flat" organizations are the model of the future.

**D**ictatorships have their advantages. I spent most of the 1980s working in communist Eastern Europe, observing firsthand countries like Romania and Russia that were run by dictators. Life was quiet and predictable back then, especially when compared to the economic and political chaos that characterizes these same nations today.

For decades all was calm and quiet in Eastern Europe, from Yugoslavia on the Western front all the way to the eastern reaches of the Soviet Empire bordering the Pacific. Quiet, calm, and *oppressed.* Dictatorships are like that. They take the fun out of life and break the human spirit that longs to soar with achievement. I can't begin to describe the dejected look of oppression that I saw in the eyes of the common workers in Eastern Europe in those years. The gleam of joy and the fierce eyes of competition were rarely seen in whole generations that grew up in those black decades.

Another label for the dictatorial style of leadership is what I call the "apostolic" view of decision-making: "I know the answers, because I have been given special insight, knowledge, and position. Therefore, I will determine our direction, for I am the leader and I know best." It amazes me that such people ever get into positions of power.

Yesterday I ran into an old friend who told me of his recent experience working under a pastor who had this kind of an attitude. He ran his church like a corporate dictator, making sure that every decision, large or tiny, was made only by him—down to personally signing all the checks. He surround-

> **Take away my people but leave my factories and soon grass will grow on the factory floor. Take away my factories but leave my people and soon we will have a new and better factory.**
>
> *—Andrew Carnegie*

ed himself with the kind of spineless yes men who would submit to this domineering style. It became a miserable place to work, and my friend finally had the joy of retiring out of the misery. Not long after my friend left that church the pastor crashed and burned in moral failure. Though he controlled everyone around him so completely, he apparently could not control his own passions.

Several times in my career I have worked for bosses like that. After I had poured countless months of energy into our cause, my work would go up in vapor because the boss just decided that we were going to do something else.

"It's been decided" is one of my least favorite phrases. It communicates that a decision was made that I had nothing to do with and that I can do nothing about. It deflates the human spirit like the mainsail going limp in the middle of a yacht race. All of a sudden one feels dead in the water, with the energies that were so focused before suddenly nowhere to be found.

### The Best Comes from the "Bottom"

At a recent employee briefing, I asked our team of sixty home office workers this question: "Where will the greatest ideas come from in our organization? Who will pioneer the greatest innovations? From what source will our great strides forward originate?" I went on to explain one of my fundamental beliefs about leadership: The greatest ideas bubble up from the workers. "They will come from *you,* not from me," I told them as they stared at me in disbelief. For some reason I don't think anyone had ever told them that before, and I'm not sure they believed me.

We know by looking at history that the greatest strides forward in any field usually come from the "radical fringe," as opposed to the institutional core. I mentioned this in the last chapter as we looked at cultivating mavericks. Very seldom does the belly of an institution bring forth great bursts of creative energy and progress in a movement. Those on the outside and on the fringes are the ones who usually come up with the best ideas.

An illustration from our kitchen shows how this principle works. Having been brought up in a German home, one of the meals we often enjoyed as children was a dish called *greisbrei* (pronounced "grease-bry"). Because my parents didn't have a lot of money when I was growing up, we had several meatless meals every week, one of them being *greisbrei,* which was basically souped-up Cream of Wheat. You bring the Cream of

> **Sydney J. Harris,**
> on dictatorial bosses:
>
> "It is impossible to learn anything important about anyone until we get him or her to disagree with us; it is only in contradiction that character is disclosed. That is why autocratic employers usually remain so ignorant about the true nature of their subordinates."
> — *Field Newspaper Syndicate*

Wheat to a boil very slowly with milk, and then add vanilla, eggs, and sugar. Once the porridge is done, you serve it with blueberries and bananas. As I have carried that tradition on to my children, they enjoy the family event of actually cooking *greisbrei* together in a huge pot on the stove.

How do you know when *greisbrei* is ready? Huge bubbles begin to arise from the bottom, exploding on the surface.

That image perfectly represents what my role as a leader is. It is to get those big bubbles to arise and burst forth on the surface of our organization. Those bubbles are the great ideas that I have to find hiding among the troops, maybe even at the bottom of the pot.

Dictators never make *greisbrei*. They never even turn the burner on. Their style is more akin to keeping the workers in the dark, with the lid on the pot.

Thomas Watson, Jr., the famous chairman of the board of IBM for many years, believed passionately that the best ideas would come from the fringes. He said, "Strangely, the expounders of many of the great new ideas of history were frequently considered on the lunatic fringe for some or all of their lives. If one stands up and is counted, from time to time one may get knocked down. But remember this: A man flattened by an opponent can get up again. A man flattened by conformity stays down for good."

## Facilitative Leadership

One big mistake dictators make is believing their own press reports. They think that the bigger they are, the more they know and the more they should control others. In reality, leadership has more to do with influencing resources. The higher I move in leadership, the more resources I must manage. The greater the leader's responsibilities, the more he or she recognizes the intrinsic worth of the followers.

This is facilitative leadership — my job is to help those I lead release as much of their potential as possible. I do not do the work; others do it under my leadership. This is a soundly biblical approach to accomplishing the work of God on earth: "He gave some [leaders] as apostles, and some as prophets, and some as evangelists, and some as pastors and teachers, for the equipping [empowering] of the saints for the work of service" (Eph. 4:11-12). God never intended those godly leaders to lord it over their charges as dictators, but to equip them to do the work that must be done:

To the elders among you, I appeal as a fellow elder. . . . Be shepherds of God's flock . . . *not lording it over those entrusted to you,* but being examples to the flock. . . . *Clothe yourselves with humility* toward one another, because, "God opposes the proud but gives grace to the humble" (1 Peter 5:1-5).

### Flattening out the Organizational Chart

Let's talk organizational charts and see how this translates to paper. Chart A shows a typical organizational chart. It is based on the domineering model that puts someone at the top controlling everything and everybody "below." This model does a great disservice, because it suggests that the more one goes "up" the organizational ladder, the more important one is and the more others are "under" that top leader responding to his or her commands.

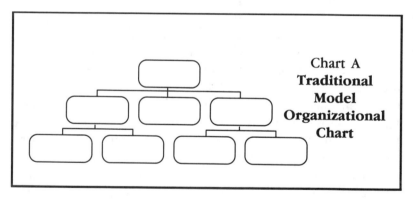

Chart A
**Traditional
Model
Organizational
Chart**

Two alternate models I have observed are found in charts B and C. Chart B is basically chart A turned horizontally, on its side. Today we have come to realize that flat, or horizontal, organizational structures are the most efficient in releasing the potential of the workers scattered throughout the organization. I like this horizontal approach because it gives the idea of "leading the charge." I, as the leader, am at the front of the troops, leading them into battle, yet I am not viewed as the dictator who dominates from the top. The leader goes first, taking others with him or her, but is not viewed as being at the top of a mighty pyramid.

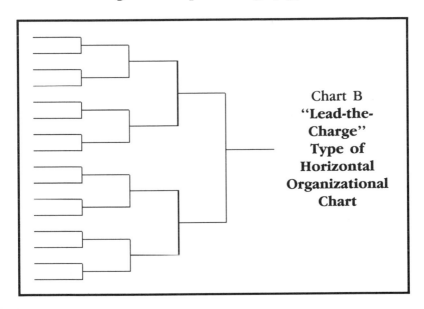

Chart B
"**Lead-the-Charge**"
**Type of Horizontal Organizational Chart**

Chart C represents a flat networking model of organization, where the leader serves a type of clearing-house function between the various players or divisions of the group. Notice that there is communication and coordination not only between the leader and each of the key players, but also among the key players themselves. The leader must not control all information, as if he or she were a central switching station.

A fourth kind of organizational chart shows leadership which probably expresses best the servant-leadership style of Jesus Christ. Chart D shows the inverted pyramid where, in fact, everything rests on the shoulders of the leader.

As I have grown in my own leadership responsibilities, I have come to realize that I bear more and more of the burdens of more and more people. Recently someone commented to me, "It must feel great to be the leader of such a large organization." I chuckled as I shared with him that in

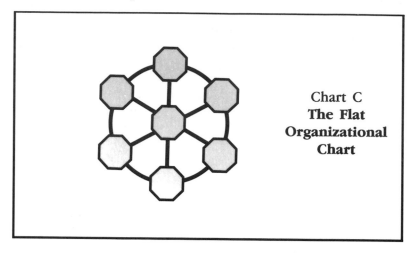

Chart C
**The Flat
Organizational
Chart**

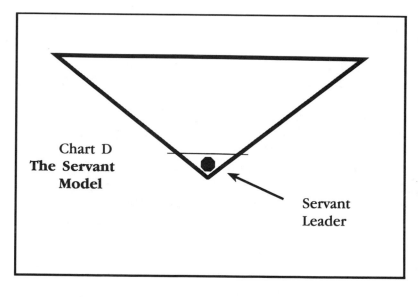

Chart D
**The Servant
Model**

Servant
Leader

fact it is not what it looks like from the outside. The higher you go in leadership, the more headaches you bear from other people's problems. A servant leader is, in fact, bearing on his or her shoulders all the people in the organization — much like one of those circus acts where they stack dozens of women on the shoulder of a super-muscleman.

---

**NEW STRUCTURES**

There has evolved a new perspective on organizational structure. Trends in business and industry emphasize the flattening of administration, the creation of more fluid and changing teams to meet changing needs, and the embedding of responsibility, accountability, and authority at all levels. New theories of management tend to shy away from organizational charts and job descriptions that represent a top-down structure in which tasks are delegated downward, authority is tightly held, and micro-managing and monitoring of performance is important. A more appropriate model is an inverted triangle with an emphasis on supporting and enabling accomplishment.

*—R. Daniel Reeves,* Ministry Advantage, *"Societal Shifts" (May/June 1993):2*

---

### Decisions Based on Dignity

Where I work we have developed a number of "core values" which help determine our decision-making style. Two of the core values speak specifically to this issue of decision-making and where ideas are going to come from:

***Individual dignity.*** We diligently maintain and promote the dignity and worth of each individual within our ministries worldwide.

"People with the proper sense of spiritual and emotional well-being are freed for productive ministry that is committed to goal-oriented planning and team accountability."

***Corporate creativity.*** We encourage creative and innovative strategies directed by the Spirit of God and implemented through policies and structures which are characterized by mutual trust and cooperation.

---

**The Ideal Supervisor**

Here's a profile of the ideal supervisor which was developed by a group of supervisors participating in a training workshop on discipline at Brookdale Hospital Medical Center.

When the supervisors were asked to identify what they "feel are the ten major functions of an effective supervisor," and to rank the functions in order of importance, they came up with the following list:

- Delegates authority in areas affecting their work.
- Consults with subordinates before making decisions pertaining to their job responsibilities.
- Gives employees the reasons for implementing decisions.
- Doesn't play favorites.
- Praises excellent work.
- Reprimands subordinates who fail to observe the proper chain-of-command relationships.
- Never reprimands or disciplines in front of coworkers.
- Encourages employees to offer their opinions and criticisms of supervisory policies.
- Listens to employees' explanations before placing blame in disciplinary situations; accepts reasonable explanations, not excuses.
- Obeys all the rules that subordinates are expected to obey.

---

In his recent book titled *Liberation Management,* Tom Peters emphasizes this strong new trend toward flat organizations. He has worked with many companies that are thriving in different industries and in different countries, and they all share one general characteristic: They are discarding the bureaucratic, hierarchical habits of the 1960s and '70s. No longer are successful organizations using hierarchies and rule books to solve their basic problems. The old model was to use rule books to try to harness hundreds of thousands of "erratic, selfish human beings" into an organization with a common purpose and to manage it in a predictable and scientific way. But those kinds of organizations become buried under their manuals and committees, having been left behind by their flat, lean rivals.

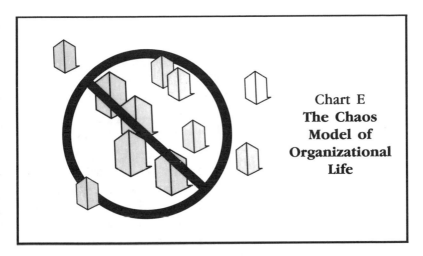

Chart E
**The Chaos Model of Organizational Life**

One word of caution, however, on this issue of diplomacy and democracy in decision-making: Don't throw out the baby with the bath water. Leaders should lead, not just implement consensus. When no one is in charge chaos ensues. I firmly believe in the need for a single person to be in charge, as opposed to a committee. A single person needs to be responsible for a specific department, project, and organization, or else the fifth model, the chaos model of chart E (that some people advocate!), will come to pass.

### Dictators Don't Lead Teams

The alternative to dictatorship in decision-making is *team leadership*. We have heard a lot about the team concept in the last couple of years. In our own organization, there is a strong movement among our field leadership groups to move toward a team emphasis. If I have heard that word once I have heard it a thousand times from the fresh young recruits. The desire to work in a team environment goes hand-in-glove with the trend away from hierarchical, top-down organizational styles. Webster defines *team* as "a number of persons associated together in work or activity; a number of persons selected to contend on one side in a match; a group of workmen each completing one of a set of operations." The word originated from the idea of a group of animals working together, as in two or more horses, oxen, or other draft animals harnessed to the same vehicle or plow. In our day we think of sports teams.

Living in Chicago, I am obviously a Chicago Bulls fan. The Bulls won three world championships under the leadership of Michael Jordan and their coach, Phil Jackson. No one doubts that the recently retired Jordan was a leader of the team. But even Michael Jordan knows that the Bulls would never have won a game without the strong support, energy, and talent of Coach Jackson and the other players—like Horace Grant, Scotty Pippen, and John Paxson.

"What makes a good manager?" someone asked Yogi Berra.

"A good ball club," Yogi replied.

> "The leaders who work most effectively, it seems to me, never say 'I.' They don't think 'I.' They think 'we.' They think 'team.' They understand their job to be making the team function. They accept the responsibility and don't sidestep, but 'we' gets the credit. There is an identification (very often, quite unconscious) with the task and with the group. This is what creates trust, what enables you to get the task done."
> —From Peter F. Drucker, Managing the Non-Profit Organization; Principles and Practice, *1990*

Leadership is teamwork, coaching, creativity—and the synergy of a group of people inspired by their leader. No one person has a corner on truth. I remember so well a frustrating time in my ministry when I was deeply troubled by what I have called the apostolic style of leadership. The apostolic style stands at the opposite end of the continuum from the leader who sees his primary role as managing the resources of a team. The apostle views truth as coming down from on high. The apostle knows the battle plan and where the team will go. It is the team's responsibility to implement the dreams and visions which were singularly presented to the leader.

That approach may sound spiritual, but I don't believe it is biblical. The age of the apostles — men like Peter and Paul, who really did receive divine inspiration — is over. A

> **You do not lead by hitting people over the head — that is assault, not leadership.**
> —*Dwight D. Eisenhower*

leader's job today is to work together with his or her team, to draw out ideas and organize them. Unless there is goal ownership, there will never be strong support for the leader. The leader will ultimately have to steer the group into fulfilling the mission, but what that mission is should be determined together by the key players of the organization.

In our organization, which we like to think is run as a Christian organization should be run, we rely on the guidance of God the Holy Spirit. We schedule times of extended prayer for our leadership team. There must be serious prayer by the leadership group if we are to discover God's will in consensus. We aren't perfect and don't always make the right decisions, but our history and track record show that we do a fair job of managing well. How do we do that, practically?

After times of prayer, we discuss major decisions and move ahead only if there is consensus. We have yet to *vote* on any decisions in our eight-member executive team, for we can sense after our discussions where we stand and if there is consensus to move ahead. If one member is strongly opposed to an idea, we either drop the proposal or put it off until a later time when more information may change opinions.

### Push Decisions Down-line whenever Possible

Rather than always dictating decisions, the good leader will try as often as possible to let those he is leading make decisions. Insisting on being in on all the decisions communicates lack of trust and confidence. It also slows the development of new leadership. Very often, *how* a project is done doesn't really matter. If it is done differently but accomplished effectively then the job gets done—which is all that matters.

I have certainly learned this in our home. One of the Finzel family rules is, Whoever is responsible to do the job can decide how it will be done. Of course we are interested in seeing the output, and we want to make sure the job is done correctly. But if I am in charge of cooking dinner tonight, then I would like to have the freedom of deciding what we will eat and how I will prepare it. Donna goes nuts if she watches me, so I send her out of the kitchen until dinner is served. It won't be done the way she does it, but she needs to relax—because I have been delegated that responsibility tonight. Actually, in our family we divide up responsibilities on a week-by-week basis, according to the responsibilities of and pressures on the various family members during that week. And he or she who does the job has the freedom to figure out how it will get done. Mark, my oldest son, does not wash my car the way I think it should be done, but I have learned to relax and accept his approach. If I watch over his shoulder and constantly correct him, all I do is deflate his confidence.

Try pushing decisions "down-line," throughout your organization. You will delight your workers. Just today I had one of my managers come to me with a decision that needed to be made

> "Leadership is the ability to recognize the special abilities and limitations of others, combined with the capacity to fit each one into the job where he will do his best."
>
> —J. Oswald Sanders,
> Spiritual Leadership,
> 1967:127

between two different options. He came to me saying, "You're the boss, and we need a decision." I could have taken two approaches. I could have given him the decision he wanted and he would have walked away and implemented my decision. But I want to empower him. Someday he may need to replace me, so he needs to have decision-making experience.

The more I can push decisions into the various departments, the more ownership and enthusiasm there will be in implementing the decisions. So I asked my manager, "This is your area and you are the professional in this area, what is your gut-level opinion about which way we should go?"

His direction was not the way I would have gone, but I decided it really didn't matter, so I told him to go with his intuition and I would back him up. He walked away from that brief interchange feeling both valuable and important in this organization. And I walked away a winner because I learned something new—as I quickly came to see, he was right . . . and I was wrong!

Harry Truman, in his typical straightforward style, once said, "A leader is a person who has the ability to get others to do what they don't want to do, and like it." But we often have the uncomfortable feeling that leaders get us to do things for their own good and not for ours. We actually suspect we are being manipulated, but we follow anyway because our jobs are on the line. Great leaders are those who truly feel that the led are just as important as the leader.

An effective leader in the new paradigm of the 1990s is Max DePree. He sums up well the ideal of nondictatorial leadership: "Leadership is—to be committed to a corporate concept of persons, the diversity of human gifts, covenantal relationships, lavish communications, including everyone, and believing that leadership is a condition of indebtedness" (Max Depree, *Leadership Is an Art*, 1989:72).

## POWERPOINTS

How dictators like to operate:
1. Hoard decisions.
2. Make decisions alone, in a vacuum.
3. View truth and wisdom as primarily their domain as the leader.
4. Restrict decisions to an elite group.
5. Surprise their workers with edicts from above.

How facilitators lead:
1. Push decisions down-line.
2. Involve others as much as possible in key decisions.
3. View truth and wisdom as being distributed throughout the organization.
4. Be a developer.
5. See their people as their greatest resource for ideas that will make them — and their people — successful.
6. Give their people space to make decisions.
7. Let those who are responsible decide how the jobs will be done.

When the best leader's work is done the people will say, "We did it ourselves!"

# Dirty Delegation
## *Refusing to Relax and Let Go*

▶ Overmanaging is one of the great
cardinal sins of poor leadership.

▶ Nothing frustrates those who work for you more than
sloppy delegation with too many strings attached.

▶ Delegation should match each worker's
follow-through ability.

It happened again yesterday. Here go the confessions of a dirty delegator. I decided that we would run a full-color half-page ad in an upcoming magazine for a special promotion. I called in Ted, my communications director, whose department is responsible for such things, and asked him to go to work on some ideas for me to consider. He went off, charged with a new project for the boss, not knowing that I was about to cut him off at the knees with my next move.

At about the same time as I gave Ted this assignment, I met an "image consultant" who wanted to do some work for us. His portfolio impressed me, so I told him about the ad project and asked him if they do those kinds of projects. "Sure, it's our specialty," he responded. I asked him to go to work on the ad—"just for ideas"—and soon received a fax from him with a great concept for the ad.

Here goes the dirty delegation, for which I should be shot: Ted called me into his office to show me the ad he had come up with on the color monitor of his Macintosh Powerbook. He had obviously put a great deal of work into the project. He had even gone down to the local library to scan ads in magazines similar to the one we were creating the ad for. "Ted," I told him with fear and trembling, "it's pretty good, but I have decided to go with the consultant's concept for the ad." In my 20/20 hindsight I realized that he had not even been aware that he was competing with someone else.

How do you think Ted felt? How would you have felt? The issue is not who did the best job on the ad. The issue is that I did not tell Ted that someone else was competing with him for the concept. I gave him the project, and then I took it back from him. And that is what dirty delegation is all about.

### Why Leaders Fail to Delegate

Snoopy is lying on top of his famous dog house. He is complaining in a whining puppy voice that everyone demands something from him. He has so much more to do than he can possibly get accomplished. In the final frame of the cartoon, Snoopy sighs, "I hate being head beagle!"

Being head beagle would be a lot easier if we could learn to spread out the work to other competent workers around us. But most leaders find it hard to let go of their precious responsibilities. They overestimate the value of the top beagle. And they underestimate the value of their followers. In fact, no leadership problem is a greater challenge than learning the fine art of clean delegation. And few leadership hang-ups create more defeated spirits as in the case I just described.

> ### Why Leaders Don't Delegate
>
> * Fear of losing authority
> * Fear of work being done poorly
> * Fear of work being done *better*
> * Unwillingness to take the necessary time
> * Fear of depending on others
> * Lack of training and positive experience

There are many reasons that delegation is hard to do well:

***Fear of losing authority.*** It takes a great deal of faith to have the courage to turn important work over to others. Those who are especially hung up with the old model of control will have a tough time learning how to delegate cleanly. Dictators never delegate, they just look for the weak-willed who can implement their every desire.

***Fear of work being done poorly.*** This is the most obvious reason why some leaders just can't bring themselves to delegate. There is fear that the responsibility will be handled poorly. In some cases such fears are

| **Delegation Works for You** |
| :---: |
| *"I'd rather get ten men to do the job than to do the job of ten men."* |
| *— D.L. Moody* |

justified—as when a heart surgeon trusts only a few nurses to assist in the stress of intricate bypass surgery. But often there is simply the hang-up of not being willing to allow others to do the work their way. In many cases, there is no perfect way to do the job, as long as the job gets done.

***Fear of work being done better.*** On the flip side, some leaders are paranoid about having subordinates show them up and do a better job than they themselves could have done. This is a sad display of pride that will eventually ruin a leader's effectiveness. Our goal is to develop new leaders who will eventually replace us (more on that in chap. 9), so we should have no worry about people working with us with skills better than our own. If you honestly believe that the best ideas flow up from below, then you must believe that some of the rank-and-file workers will do some work better than you do. A leader should surround himself or herself with specialists who can each do their particular job much better than their supervisor.

***Unwillingness to take the necessary time.*** Delegation takes time. Task-oriented people tend to want to just get the job done instead of waiting on others to do it through delegation. I can often do a job better and faster if I do it myself. If I take the time to delegate I first have to meet with the person, then I have to explain what I want, then I have to wait on them to have the time to do the project . . . and I have to hope that when I finally get the job back, it will be according to my standards!

*Fear of depending on others.* This problem comes right on the heels of the impatience just described. It is the issue of leadership independence — which some people find very hard to give up. They have grown so independent and are so aggressive that they cannot learn to

> "The best executive is the one who has sense enough to pick good men to do what he wants done, and self-restraint enough to keep from meddling with them while they do it."
>
> — *Theodore Roosevelt*

depend on others in a team environment, where the whole task is not completed until each member does his or her part.

*Lack of training and positive experience.* Perhaps for some leaders the issue is that they have never been trained in the fine art of delegating. No one has shown them how, no one has ever believed in them enough to delegate to them, so they have learned to work as independents doing their own work. If this is your experience, then you should begin with small experiments at delegating tasks to others that you would normally do yourself. Try it . . . and see how you can multiply your effectiveness!

**Delegation Is Giving the Pride of Personal Ownership**
As we have seen, some of the greatest lessons of poor leadership come from the ineptitude of communist regimes before the fall of the Iron Curtain. This is particularly true in this issue of delegation. Delegation is about "private owner-

ship" of one's work, and in the communist system there simply was no private ownership. No one took pride in his or her work . . . and, therefore, nothing got accomplished. After seventy years of communism, you find in formerly communist nations a completely failed infrastructure that is impossible to rebuild. I feel sorry for those millions who are paying the price today for the decades of tyranny that denied men and women the simple freedom of job ownership and private enterprise.

Just to illustrate the power of personal ownership of private property, take the example of how food was produced in the former Soviet Union. More than 90 percent of farming was done on collective farms, but those farms produced only 10 percent of

> **The Four Stages of Delegation**
>
> 1. **Assignment**
> 2. **Authority**
> 3. **Accountability**
> 4. **Affirmation**

the food consumed. Crops on the collective farms rotted in the fields because there was no one to harvest them. One Iowa farmer who owns his own land could outproduce a collective farm that employed hundreds of workers on land many times larger. Why? Pride of ownership and personal control.

Where did the bulk of the Soviet Union's best food come from? Some, of course, was imported from the West — including yearly doses of wheat from the good old Midwestern farmers of America. But almost half of the fresh food supply for the population came from tiny private plots that citizens were allowed to own. Those little plots rimmed the perimeters of many a Russian city, and with every spare minute private citizens worked those parcels as the only real expression of what they themselves were able to accomplish — beyond the all-encompassing reach of the government.

In the same way we must give our workers freedom to own their work, or they will lose the pride of personal accomplishment and their productivity will quickly wane.

### How to Take the Wind out of Their Sails

Overmanaging is one of the greatest sins of leadership. We must be careful not to micro-manage people to death. Delegation means giving people the freedom to decide how jobs will be done. Dirty delegation is constantly looking over the shoulders of those asked to do the work. It is confining and restricting to the creativity and problem-solving potential that longs to come out of most people. It is also making decisions behind the backs of those to whom work is delegated.

"OK, Sam, here is what I want you to do," our boss told my good friend who was new on the scene in an organization I worked for. "You're bright: study this problem and come up with a solution that we can use to fix it."

That's all Sam wanted to hear. He was like a hungry Doberman that had just been tossed a fresh steak. He tackled the assignment with all the gusto you can expect from an eager young recruit. He dug in, turned on, rolled up his sleeves, and went to work.

Among the many things running through his mind, Sam wanted to: (a) make a great impression by showing his boss that he was even brighter than rumored, and, (b) get off to a great start by helping solve a major challenge that had been plaguing us for months. He studied and researched the problem, explored possible options, and over the next months pounded out an impressive

---

**Four Questions Every Follower Asks**

What am I supposed to do?
Will you let me do it?
Will you help me when I need it?
Will you let me know how I'm doing?

—*Dr. Lorne Sanny,*
*The Business Ministry Journal,*
*1992*

---

report on his keyboard. I recall the final product being close to fifty impressive pages.

Sam had been given a long lead time to complete the project. When it was finally finished the fateful day came for him to deliver his first work of art to his new boss. With great pride and a sense of fulfillment he placed the document in the boss' in-box. And he waited . . . and waited. Hearing nothing, after several days he finally got the courage to stop his boss in the hallway and ask him about the report. "Looks good, Sam," he said almost off-the-cuff, "but we've decided to take another approach with that project."

What? Did he hear what he thought he heard? Can you hear the air rushing out of his bubble as his ego completely deflated? To say that Sam was crushed, angered, and puzzled would be to put it mildly. How would you have reacted? Can you feel the rage that Sam felt that day? How many mistakes did this leader make with Sam? I can think of several outrageous ones:

***Lack of empathy with the enlisted folks.*** The longer you lead, the less you remember what it was like to follow. For some there may never have been a chance to really feel what followers feel. People who hold great power in organizations usually don't sense their power—like a skunk who is immune to the aroma that has so much power over others! Leaders lead . . . and followers cringe!

***Failure to "give" work to others.*** This leader never really "gave" the project to Sam at all. He teased Sam like you would tease a dog with a bone that you have no intention of giving him. He showed a great lack of respect by giving Sam the project and then taking it back without ever bothering to let him know. First comes the assignment, then the authority. And with that authority must come the freedom to get the job done and the respect to follow through with respect for the dignity of that worker.

***Failure to stay in touch.*** The next classic mistake Sam's boss made is that he never bothered to check up on how

Sam was doing. Had he known how Sam was killing himself to do this project right, he would have seen the sense of ownership that had taken over Sam's emotions, and he would have been tuned in to the problem that was looming on the horizon.

***Short-circuiting the decision-making process.*** Sam was simply out of any loop in the decision-making process. In fact, once a decision about the project was made, he wasn't even informed.

But he was not alone, for no communication system was in place for people to know when big decisions were made behind closed doors. More on that in chapter 7, on communication chaos.

***Playing the inner-circle game.*** Who really made the decision about scuttling Sam's project? The boss and his private inner circle of top management. I've seen quite a few organizations—yes, even Christian ministries—that pride themselves on running a "Bible-centered" operation, while in fact holding to a double standard when it comes to information flow.

They boast equality and transparency in the fellowship of the family of faith, but in fact keep many parts of that family in the dark. I know that certain information must be kept confidential, but that is not the problem here. Sam never got a real honest hearing. The boss and the inner circle decided that they knew the answers they wanted before the project came to fruition.

By the way, what do you think this incident did to Sam the eager beaver? Yes, it took all the wind out of his sails. He tossed out the respect he had for his leader, and he pulled into a shell that he maintains to this day. From that day on he decided that his number-one goal in the organizations was his own self-preservation—not the good of the ministry. He told me, and I quote, "I will *never* volunteer to do a project for him again, period."

### The Great Delegation

Delegation is seen throughout the Old and New Testaments of the Bible. One thinks almost automatically of Nehemiah and the thousands of workers to whom he delegated responsibilities as they rebuilt the walls of Jerusalem. Or there's Aaron, brother of Moses, who was put in charge of the camp while Moses spent his extended times in the presence of God on Mount Sinai. Aaron is in fact a good example of delegated responsibility that goes bad, for he failed in his duties and Moses came back to a mess. That is the risk we take when we delegate.

In the New Testament the most profound example is Jesus' delegating to His disciples the fulfillment of the Great Commission. In fact, notice how God the Father delegated the authority for salvation to the Son, Jesus Christ, and He in turn passed on that authority to His disciples:

> All authority in heaven and on earth has been given to Me. Therefore go and make disciples of all nations, baptizing them in the name of the Father and of the Son and of the Holy Spirit, and teaching them to obey everything I have commanded you. And surely I am with you always, to the very end of the age (Matt. 28:18-20).

Notice also that the Son promised to follow up on that delegation by His presence: "Surely I am with you always." He is going to hold His followers accountable, but He also intends to encourage them along the way. Excellent practice of delegation!

After just three short years of preparation, Jesus was counting on His disciples to fulfill the mandate of His revolution and spread the Gospel to the ends of the earth. He trusted them so completely that He had no "plan B backup." They would build the church and start a worldwide movement . . . or it just would not happen. There were no backup plans lying in wait behind closed doors in some other secret division of His enterprise.

I think the twelve disciples knew that they were it, and that Jesus believed in them so completely that He had no other plan. Thus they gave themselves to the Commission with reckless abandon and devotion, even to the point of death. It is amazing what followers will do for the leader who shows this level of faith in them.

In the second generation of Christ's followers, the Apostle Paul stands out as again seeing the importance of delegating. Near the end of his life Paul laid out his delegation strategy for completing the task of building the New Testament church:

> You then, my son, be strong in the grace that is in Christ Jesus. And the things you have heard me say in the presence of many witnesses entrust to reliable men who will also be qualified to teach others (2 Tim. 2:1-2).

Paul is asking those to whom he delegated the task of spreading the Gospel to delegate it on down the line to a third and fourth layer of workers. That is good delegation — passing the authority and responsibility throughout the enterprise.

### Follow-through Styles that You Should Know

An important principle that many leaders stumble on is the need to recognize that different kinds of followers need different styles of supervision. Once I have delegated a responsibility, I must practice various forms of supervision and accountability according to the condition of the follower.

I can best explain the difference with illustrations of two very different people I delegate work to, and how they respond. One is named Andrew, and is my five-year-old son. The other is named Joe, and is decades older and wiser.

Andrew falls on the low end of what I call the "delegation

continuum" (see chart on this page). I have been trying to train him in "KP" in our family. "KP" stands for "kitchen police," and the four children have a rotating system whereby on certain days of the week they have KP. The responsibilities include such things as setting the table for dinner, clearing the table after dinner, and taking out the garbage. Andrew has very low motivation, interest, or skill for this job, and thus I have to constantly hover over him to get him to do it. Not only do I have to constantly remind him to do his work, but I have to help him and show him how. If I leave him alone, the chances are very good that the system will break down. Andrew needs close and constant supervision of a very specific nature. And some of the people who work with you and for you will be in the same category.

Then there is Joe, who has worked for me for over a year on a very demanding special project for our organization. I live in Chicago where our headquarters are, but he lives in California, far away from my daily personal supervision. But that's no problem, because Joe is the ultimate self-directed worker—he gets the job done on autopilot. He never misses deadlines and does a fabulous job at what he does. What is the difference between Andrew and Joe? Not only age, but motivation, interest, and skill.

There is a continuum of follow-through ability, as expressed in this chart:

---

**The Delegation Continuum:**
**The Follow-through Styles of Different Workers**

◆----------------------------------------------------------------◆

| Low Interest | High Interest |
| Low Motivation | High Motivation |
| Low Skill | High Skill |

---

This practice of varying your style of supervision according to your followers' follow-through style could be called situational leadership. One of the best books I have come across on the fine art of delegating and supervising is Hersey and Blanchard's *Management of Organizational Behavior*. They introduce the idea of situational leadership, and show that there are four ways of delegating and keeping up with those to whom work has been assigned, based on their own maturity and motivation. These four leadership alternatives are *delegating, participating, selling,* and *telling* (Hersey and Blanchard, 1982). The greatest mistake we can make in supervising is to treat everyone the same. Hersey and Blanchard describe these four different supervision styles:

*Delegating.* This is the best kind of supervision for the person who, like Joe, is self-directed and highly skilled at his or her task.

*Participating.* This is the kind of situation where the leader is working with the follower. The leader literally shows the follower how to get the job done. When I taught my oldest son how to cut our lawn, the first season we did it together. Now he can do it totally on his own while I am out of town. I moved with him from the participating to the delegating category.

*Selling.* Here the people have high skill but low motivation. They will do the job best if you can sell them on doing it. This is a task we who work in nonprofit organizations have to practice day after day.

*Telling.* This is the approach I take with Andrew and my other children (except my daughter, who for some reason enjoys KP!) since they have low interest, low motivation, and low skill. With some people, you must strongly tell them that they must do a job whether they like it or not. This is the lowest form of delegation, and should be used as little as possible.

Here is the Delegation Continuum chart, now adding the situational leadership styles to the equation:

---

### The Delegation Continuum:
### The Follow-through Styles of Different Workers

◆----------------------------------------------------------------------------------◆

| Low Interest | High Interest |
| Low Motivation | High Motivation |
| Low Skill | High Skill |

Telling ------ Selling ------ Participating ------ Delegating

---

### Let's Play "Pass the Monkey"

Back in the 1950s, The *Harvard Business Review* ran an article about delegation and monkeys, from which the expression arose, "get that monkey off my back." In that fascinating account the writer described a typical scenario that is repeated daily in our office and in organizations across the country and around the world. Every time you give a job to someone, picture yourself putting a monkey on their back. It is their responsibility to care for and feed that monkey until it's time to set it free—that is, until the task is completed. It sounds simple but it's not. One of my coworkers comes into my office with a problem about a responsibility which has been delegated to him or her. There seems to be a snag and he needs help. That worker's goal is to get that monkey to climb off his or her back and onto mine. How do I get the monkey? By saying something like, "Well, let me give it some thought," or, "Let me talk to some others about it," or, "Well, maybe I can handle it." What I have done is relieved that person of his or her monkey. I have taken responsibility for its care and feeding.

If this process repeats itself several times a day, you can get the picture. I have an office full of monkeys that are really the responsibilities of other people. I am more than happy to have an open-door policy and to help my colleagues with their problems. But I have an imaginary sign over my doorway as you look out of my office that reads, "Did they take their monkey with them?"

Don't do other people's work for them. That is my natural temptation, just like when I ask my children to do a job that I used to do and normally do. I must cultivate greater independence and responsibility, by giving them a job and letting them do it. Not long ago I asked my son to wash my car after school. He was looking forward to it but, to his dismay, I arrived home that evening with a newly washed vehicle. "What happened, Daddy?" he asked with great surprise and disappointment. I had to confess to him that I was practicing dirty delegation again. I figured it was easier to run it through the car wash on the way home than to have him take an hour and do an inferior job. In that case, I preferred the easier route to setting the monkey free.

## POWERPOINTS

This issue of delegation is an issue of respect. With responsibility must come the authority to do a job. I believe in the 80/20 rule of success. Eighty percent of the time I'll make the right decision, and 20 percent of the time I will make mistakes or not do it as good as it could have been done. I allow my subordinates the freedom of the 80/20 rule as well, and give them the grace and room to fail.

My rule of thumb is this: *He who is asked to do the job plans how it will be done.* We can check our workers' progress, but we should not, (a) constantly look over their shoulders, (b) tell them how to do their work, (c) reject their work in favor of our "expert" approach, nor, (d) reverse their strategy decisions simply for ones we might favor as leaders.

Key Ingredients for Clean Delegation:
1. *Faith* in the one to whom you delegate.

2. *Release* from the desire to do it better yourself.
3. *Relaxation* from the obsession that it has to be done your way.
4. *Patience* in the desire to do it faster yourself.
5. *Vision* to develop others with your delegation freedom.

Guidelines for Clean Delegation:
1. Choose qualified people.
2. Exhibit confidence.
3. Make their duties clear.
4. Delegate the proper authority.
5. Do not tell them how to do the work.
6. Set up accountability points along the way.
7. Supervise according to their follow-through style.
8. Give them room to fail occasionally.
9. Give praise and credit for work well done.

# Communication Chaos
## *Singing off the Same Page in the Hymnbook*

▶ Never assume that *anyone* knows *anything.*

▶ The bigger the group, the more attention must be given to communication.

▶ When left in the dark, people tend to dream up wild rumors.

▶ Communication must be the passionate obsession of effective leadership.

This past summer I introduced my children to Yellowstone National Park for the first time. I had not been there myself since I was a child, and had forgotten how vast America's most famous national park really is. Amid the beauty of Yellowstone was one sad blemish that shocked us: the many scars of the forest fires that destroyed much of the park in 1989. And in those ashes was the story of a communication disaster that almost caused more damage than the fire itself.

It seems that the employees of the private company that runs the concessions in Yellowstone Park became worried for their lives during the height of the fires that threatened to ravage the entire park that summer. As the fires grew more and more dangerous, the rumor began to circulate that the executives of the concession company had a secret escape plan to get out of danger if the fires got too close. Information spread that the employees would have to fend for themselves. It wasn't long before the company had a near mutiny on their hands, since they were seen as taking care of themselves first and the employees only second, if at all.

Lack of communication on evacuation plans, coupled

with the unfounded rumor, destroyed confidence in the company's good will. After learning of the problem, the company hired a forest service spokesman who brought daily updates on the status of the fire to all employees. Included in the communications was a detailed explanation of evacuation plans that all employees were a part of. The company had no executive escape plan, and the leadership had fully intended to make sure that every employee was safe amid the disaster. But that was not communicated, so the employees were left to speculate.

> **Nothing happens until people talk.**

Rumor mills are part and parcel of every work group. Rumors often spread like a forest fire, and rarely if ever are anywhere close to reality. Perhaps it was foolish for those Yellowstone employees to believe such a heartless rumor, but when things get bad and survival is involved, people can begin to create their own reality—if the true reality is not communicated.

*Never assume that anyone knows anything.* This is a core leadership principle. We can never communicate enough in our organizations. Like the pulsing red cells rushing through our veins keeping our bodies alive, communication systems are the lifeblood of organizations. The folks at the far extremities desperately need to know what is going on in the minds of those at the leadership center, if they are to feel comfortable, safe, and knowledgeable about their work.

Though much of my job as a CEO is communicating our vision and selling our dream out there among the public constituents, my insiders need to hear from me just as much if not more. In fact, I expend as much energy on internal as on external communications. I never assume anymore that even my closest associates can read my mind—I've learned too much watching false information spread.

**How to Know You Have a Communication Hang-up**

A gentleman was walking down a residential street and noticed a man struggling with a washing machine at the doorway of his house. When he volunteered to help the homeowner was overjoyed, and the two men together began to work and struggle with the bulky appliance. After several minutes of fruitless effort the two stopped and just looked at each other. They were on the verge of total exhaustion. Finally, when they caught their breath, the first man said to the homeowner: "We'll never get this washing machine in there!" To which the homeowner replied: "In? I'm trying to move it out!"

Communication chaos begins when small groups start getting larger. As long as the organization is small, oral communication is sufficient and generally everyone knows everything. But as things grow larger, the need for more formal communication grows. You'll recall the chart from chapter 4 on the life cycles of organizations. I have included it again here in a slightly different form. I have displayed the process from birth to maturity, without the decline toward death. As organizations grow from small entrepreneurships into professionally managed organizations, communication must be given more attention and must become more formal.

---

**The Life Cycles of Organizations**

| Birth | Adolescence | Maturity |
|-------|-------------|----------|

$\longrightarrow$

**Communication Patterns**

| | | |
|-------|---|----------|
| Oral | | Written |
| Informal | | Formal |
| Spontaneous | | Planned |
| Active | | Passive |
| Lively | | Liturgical |

A number of years ago I had the exciting opportunity to be in on the ground floor of a new organization. We were a group of zealous entrepreneurs who were creating something out of nothing. There were only five families involved, and we started out in borrowed space in the basement of an office building. I remember vividly how we would make decisions in the hallways and communicate orally from one open office door to the other. That approach worked great and we were off and running. There was no question about which page of the hymnbook we were singing from.

But five years down the road we had grown to a staff of more than sixty, and had taken over the entire building. The organization had taken on a life of its own. The style of decision-making that worked so easily at first now created chaos and frustration throughout the organization. "Hallway decision-making" became the negative label for poor communications. That which had worked so well informally now had to be formalized.

One reason the informal broke down was that newcomers to the group were left in the dark. The same small band kept making all the decisions orally, and no paper trail was left for others to trace.

As organizations grow, the original group of founders can become an inside elite. Since they were there from the beginning, they have the most information and power. Newcomers feel left out and in the dark. I recall one of the new employees in our group complaining about the lack of information in this vivid fashion: "I feel like a part of a mushroom farm—I'm left completely in the dark and fed more manure from time to time." That was a revealing statement of the kind of pain that can be caused by poor communication.

### Exactly Where Are We Going Anyway?
Orchestra conductors have the unique ability to bring harmony out of chaos. For a number of years Donna and I lived in one of the cultural capitals of Europe—Vienna, Austria.

What a privilege that was. One of the highlights of our social life was to go down to the Philharmonic Hall and enjoy the beautiful Vienna Philharmonic Orchestra. Musicians consider the hall where the Philharmonic meets to be the most acoustically perfect music hall anywhere in the world. And I don't know of a better symphony orchestra than the Vienna Philharmonic. However, when the orchestra first comes out and begins tuning, their sounds amaze you by their discord and chaos. How can this noise become beautiful music? The answer lies in the conductor. He walks out onto the stage, steps onto his platform, taps his music stand, and gives the artists the *A* note. All of his leadership is wrapped up in that *A* note, where harmony flows out of chaos.

Back to my experience with the organization that grew from a small, elite group to a large family of workers: About five years into the project, we were beginning to sense growing pains. We invited a management consultant to come in and spend a day with our top leadership. We sat in a circle around a large conference room table and began to talk about basic fundamentals of the organization.

The consultant asked us each to write down on a sheet of paper the core purpose of our organization. Then we went around the circle and read what we had written. No two of us said the same thing, and some of us were far afield from the others! No wonder there was so much chaos among us! Like the strings of a guitar

> The two words *information* and *communication* are often used interchangeably, but they signify quite different things. Information is *giving out;* communication is *getting through.*
>
> — *Sydney J. Harris,*
> *Publishers-Hall Syndicate*

that lose their tuning, we had lost our harmony as a leadership group. You know you're in trouble when your top leadership is confused about such fundamental issues as the basic purpose for the group's existence!

Our underlying problem was the failure to make the shift

from an *oral* planning mode to a more formal *written* one. It was time we sharpened our strategic plan in writing so that we could all sign off on it and could then use that body of knowledge to orient each new member of the group. When the group is small, everyone knows the score because everyone has time to touch base with each other almost on a daily basis. But if your group grows, you as the leader cross a threshold where you can no longer physically stay in touch through informal means. In our case, we began to have people in other cities and countries as part of our organization. There was no way that the oral tradition could continue to drive the operation.

Sooner or later you must put your plans down in writing and spell out your direction clearly. That doesn't mean that the plans won't change, but it does mean that everyone knows the rules of the game; it means that you're all trying to conquer the same mountain.

### Communication: A Series of Linkages

The higher you go in leadership, the more sensitive you have to be about everything you communicate. I call this becoming aware of "communication linkages." Every time I make a phone call or write a letter or make a decision, I have to ask, "What people are affected by this decision/letter/memo/directive? What are the linkages?" It can drive me crazy to think of all the people who need to be informed when a decision is made. Sometimes I feel like a fly caught in a spider web—tangled and stuck because of all the sticky communication lines attached to me! But I know that the consequences of not informing everyone is communication chaos and damaged relationships. Invariably, I send copies of memos or letters to various other people to make sure that they are aware of my decisions and actions.

Not only must you communicate clearly the decision you make, quite often you must clear those decisions with a number of colleagues before finalizing them. Even though I have authority to make decisions in my organization, I would damage the entire system by unilaterally doing so without conferring with the key individuals involved.

Let me give a case in point. We have a gentleman who has been working for us for more than thirty-five years, based in Manila. Just five years short of retirement, he is looking for a new challenge. I am very interested in deploying him to Moscow, to help us develop our work in that part of the world which is booming with new opportunities. This is what I call internal recruitment, where an insider is recruited from one part of the organization to work in another.

He went to Moscow this past summer, to "test the waters," and explore ministry possibilities. He came back exuberant and excited. However, I cannot unilaterally redeploy him without taking into account his previous supervisor who oversaw his work in the Philippines, and his potential new supervisor who oversees our work in Europe. The entire process must be coordinated with all of the principal parties involved. And that is the hard work of effective communication.

> ### The Communication Life Blood
>
> "A corporation's values are its life's blood. Without effective communication, actively practiced, without the art of scrutiny, those values will disappear in a sea of trivial memos and impertinent reports.
>
> "There may be no single thing more important in our efforts to achieve meaningful work and fulfilling relationships than to learn and practice the art of communication."
>
> —*Max DePree*
> Leadership Is an Art,
> *1989:108*

### When New Leaders Change the Rules

There is never a time when more in-house communication is needed than when you first become a leader. People need to know what to expect of their new boss. My recent appointment to my current leadership role meant taking over an organization that had been run with one particular leadership style for twenty-two years. Then I come in, with the perspective of a new generation and new ideas about what is important and how work is to be done. How does that play with my employees? It makes them very uneasy and nervous, because they don't know what to expect. So, communication has become a supremely important part of my new job. Just like when a new coach takes over: The team has the right to know how we're going to play ball.

### Effective Leaders Are Avid Listeners

Leaders often love to talk. They enjoy listening to their own great pearls of wisdom and insight. Sometimes they even begin to believe their own press reports. And as they gain more authority, they have less reason to listen to subordinates. Have you ever noticed that there is much more horizontal communication in an organization than vertical? Coworkers are always talking about everything, but the communications between those coworkers and their superiors are much less frequent and much more formal. Leaders must figure out ways to tap into that underground flow of information. They must "keep current on the undercurrents."

The more people you lead, the more you must listen. Effective leadership has more to do with *listening* than with talking. Leaders by their very nature tend to be removed from the front lines of battle in the organization. Therefore, they *must* listen to those who are in the trenches, and rely on that information to make wise decisions. Yet the pressures of leadership work against that process at every turn.

Here are some of the reasons why it is hard for leaders to listen to everyone in the organization:

*Too little time.* The more people you lead, the less time you have for each person. (And, of course, the more tasks each of them expects you to accomplish!)

*Too many people.* There are literally dozens of leaders in our organization with whom I should have an intimate relationship—including the seven administrators in the home office, the leaders of our six field offices in North America, and the forty-plus leaders of our works around the world. There are just too many of them, but they can each get individually frustrated with me if I don't take the time or build the systems whereby they can communicate with me.

*Pressure.* Leaders usually find themselves under a constant sense of pressure from more deadlines and responsibilities than they can handle. The image of a soldier in battle comes to mind: Here I stand in the trenches, with bullets flying, planes buzzing overhead, and tanks rolling in our direction. My radio is crackling with news from many fronts. Then along comes one of my people who wants a quiet, long talk about his or her concerns. The intense pressures of leadership sometimes make it very difficult to listen attentively— which brings us back to chapter 2 and making time for people.

*Distance.* In some cases the sheer problem of physical distance between the leader and his or her followers makes it tough to stay in close contact.

*Too much knowledge.* Leaders sometimes know so much that they find it hard to listen to someone rehearsing stories, facts, or anecdotes that the leader has already heard dozens of times.

*Pride.* This comes on the heels of the knowledge problem: Sometimes we simply think we know too much. We get to the place where we don't think we can learn from others. The admonition of Scripture should be clear enough: "Be quick to listen but slow to speak" (see James 1:19).

*Communication overload.* This problem was addressed in the chapter on paperwork versus peoplework. The telecommunications revolution is tightening the information noose around the neck of the average leader. Leaders can become so saturated with communication that they find their system shutting down from overload. With cellular phones, notebook computers, faxes, E-mail, and now PDAs (personal digital assistants), you can run but you can't hide from communication overload!

Nothing stops the progress of an organization more quickly than leaders failing to listen. Like hardening of the arteries, hardening of the categories and a closed mind will destroy a leader's credibility. Followers want to communicate to their leaders. If you fail to listen to them, their very effectiveness and job satisfaction will be in jeopardy.

### The Price of Leadership Isolation

Here are several real-life, anonymous accounts from wounded soldiers who lost respect for leaders who didn't bother to listen. First, a young woman hurt by a leader who constantly cut her off:

Our leader was a very "choleric" person. We followers were really hurt by him many times. We expected he would wait and give us answers to our serious questions about our work. Many times, he walked off when we were mid-sentence, having heard nothing. This happened to women more than men.

Then, the account of a youth director in a church, who was called on the carpet with no warning:

While attending college I accepted a youth director's position as a local church. I dedicated approximately twenty to thirty hours a week working with junior and senior highers. After serving the Lord there for two years I was called into an elders meeting. One of the elders, who had three children in my ministry—growing in the Lord—took out a list of all the things I had done wrong in the past two years. Most of what they said was true, for I was brand new in this work and made lots of mistakes. The next thing I knew, the elders were calling for my resignation in the heated emotions of the meeting. It came as a complete surprise. What did I learn? (1) I cannot think of one instance in those two years that any of the elders or the pastor shepherded me in my ministry. (2) I had no idea nor warning that I was doing anything wrong. (3) Leaders and staff had no significant relationships.

And here is a letter from a frustrated follower stationed overseas, who found himself stuck with a leader who had no interest in listening:

Our local committee was voting on an issue. The majority of the leadership was in favor of the action, but the committee chairman was against it. As the votes were cast and didn't go his way, he gave a new explanation of the issue. We took another vote, with the same results. But he wouldn't give in until we voted six more times, always with the same results. It was a frustrating experience!

Certainly, if followers have a bill of rights, the right to be heard by their leader must be Article Number One. I believe in strong leadership, but also in a strong leader who listens. Assuming that the group in that last example had a democratic process of decision-making, the leader should have been in touch with the people enough to know where the decision was going. The incident just shows how out of touch he was with his followers.

### Communicate the Big Picture with Passion
Communication is especially important in the larger issues of corporate life. I encourage leaders to spell out their purposes, key goals, and core values, and to "preach them

from the housetops." In fact, preaching the purpose and core values of an organization is one of the essential jobs of leaders. The workers who have been around a long time need to be reminded, and the new recruits need to be "enfolded" into the corporate vision.

Here are two recent examples from organizations that clearly communicate to newcomers exactly what they stand for. The first is from an organization called *Church Resource Ministries,* led by Dr. Sam Metcalf and based in Fullerton, California.

### The Expectations and Privileges of CRM Staff

As a staff person with CRM, it is fair for me to expect the following from those whom I follow throughout the organization. I can expect:

***To know those who lead me and what they believe.***
If I follow you, will I know who you are? What are you like? Are you authentic . . . honest . . . and will you deal with me with integrity?

***To have leaders who will explain to me their vision.***
What do you see for me? What's the future and how do I fit? Do you care about my future? Will you have a place for me or will you simply use me?

***To never be left in isolation.***
Are you there for me? Do you love me . . . will you love me? Do you care about my cares . . . my concerns . . . my needs?

***To be heard.***
To whom will you listen? Will I be heard . . . taken seriously . . . and appreciated?

***To be trusted.***
Can I take initiative without fear? Will my creativity be

rewarded and encouraged? Will I be respected?

### *To be provided a context for growth.*
Will I be encouraged to be a lifelong learner? Will my gifts be increasingly identified and expressed? Can I live in a context where God's power can be freely manifested in my life? Will I be developed?

### *To be held accountable.*
Will I be held accountable for personal godliness and holiness in all aspects of life and ministry? Will I be fairly evaluated for the performance of my responsibilities? Will I be lovingly held to God's best for my life?

### *To be the object of grace.*
Will I be forgiven, even in the face of shortcomings, inadequacies, and failure? Will I have the freedom to be whom God has made me? Will I be led with kindness?

The second example is from one of the most successful companies in America, one that has truly placed God first in its business. Several months ago I had the opportunity to visit the national headquarters of the ServiceMaster Corporation. No one at ServiceMaster would ever be foggy about what the chief goals and vision of that organization are. It is literally plastered on the walls of their corporate offices.

Anyone considering becoming a partner with the Service-Master family—which is what they call their employees—is expected to be committed to their corporate values:

### ServiceMaster

We are in the business of serving others. This requires all of us to have an unending pursuit of excellence as we bring the benefit of our extraordinary service to our customers. This way of doing business can be best expressed by our four objectives. They are:

To honor God in all that we do.
To help people develop.
To pursue excellence.
To grow profitably.

### The Nuts and Bolts of Clear Communication

Clearing up the chaotic communication in an organization is not easy. If you are building a new group from scratch, it is much easier. Whether you are starting over or are trying to be more faithful in clearing up cloudy communications, there are four basic areas where your followers need to be clear:

*The vision and values of the group.* Every group needs a clear mission statement indicating the strategic purpose of the organization. This mission statement is a clear declaration of vision. In addition to the mission/purpose statement, there should be an agreed-upon set of clearly defined goals and objectives. This organizational blueprint needs to be communicated clearly, and updated as often as the nature of your work changes.

We'll take a closer look at the whole area of corporate values and culture in the next chapter, and at vision in chapter 10.

*The chain of command.* If one of your people has a question or problem, do they know who handles what in your organization? If they have a serious complaint, is there a clear path for their issues to rise up to the top? When you have a project to assign within the group, do you know whose job it should be? If there is a major problem, do you know who is in charge of that area? These are all issues of chain of command. Chain of command is simply the orderly dividing up of responsibilities within the organization, and making sure everyone knows who is responsible for what. Chain of command clarifies the questions of *who reports to whom, who supervises whom,* and *who is in change of what.*

***Organizational charts.*** We have looked at organizational charts at length in previous chapters. Organizational charts are an important part of clear communication. The idea of an organizational chart is not really new. Moses had a very detailed one. Does your group have an organizational chart? It is helpful for everyone in an organization to know where they fit. The "org chart" is a *people map,* outlining the relationships within the organization. It shows the lines of authority and responsibility. It enables everyone to visualize the chain of command.

Organizational charts help leadership see, in a quick, visual overview, just how the work of their company is organized. The charts also help the members of the organization know where they fit, and where to go in the organization for help, resources, permissions, clearances, complaints, and grievances. They are also very helpful in explaining the corporate culture to the new members of your group. Organizational charts show the full scope of relationships in organizational life. Since those relationships change often, the charts should change as often as necessary. They should be simple and they should be flexible, but most of all, they should *be.*

***Job descriptions.*** Do your people have job descriptions? There are a thousand ways to write job descriptions, some quite complex and others very simple. I like job descriptions that lean toward simplicity. They need to be flexible and should outline three basic ingredients of any job: (1) What are your primary responsibilities in the organization? (2) What key activities and tasks are you asked to do to fulfill those responsibilities? (3) To whom do you report? With a clear job description, there can be no confusion between the leader and the follower about what that person is supposed to be doing. And it becomes the primary tool for evaluating effectiveness in an annual review system.

## POWERPOINTS

How do you know if your organization has communication chaos? Ask yourself how many of these symptoms are present:

1. Chaos and confusion about the group's direction
2. Arguments or disagreements about priorities
3. Duplication of effort
4. Waste of resources through jobs that get canceled midstream
5. Conflicts among departments
6. Poor morale
7. Poor productivity
8. Idleness of resources
9. Job insecurity

*There are no little people in your organization.* Years ago, Francis Schaeffer wrote a significant book titled *No Little People.* He argued that in God's kingdom there are no little people and no little places. I think the same principle should be practiced by Christian leaders in their attitudes about the far-flung corners of their organizations. Everyone is important. Everyone has a right and a need to know what is going on in the organization — the big news as well as the little details. The more people are informed, the more they feel a part of the whole organization and the less chance there is for misunderstanding.

How do you feel if others know something you don't know? Have you ever learned significant news about your own organization from an outsider? How does that make you feel? Insignificant? Hurt? Forgotten? Keep the troops informed. Have a passion to communicate, communicate, communicate. One really cannot over-communicate. Listen to the advice of Max DePree, from *Leadership Is an Art:*

> The right to know is basic. Moreover, it is better to err on the side of sharing too much information than risk leaving someone in the dark. Information is power, but it is pointless power if hoarded. Power must be shared for an organization or a relationship to work (Depree, 1989:104–5).

***How to avoid fossilization.*** As you looked at the chart on life cycles and communicaton at the beginning of this chapter, you may have thought, *I don't want us to become fossilized in the formal rituals of bureaucracy.* Here are a few tips to keep the life in your growing organization, as you commit more and more communication into written form:

- ☑ Keep memos brief.
- ☑ Include one-page summaries on the top of lengthy reports.
- ☑ Use faxes and E-mail to keep communication fresh and up-to-the-minute.
- ☑ Produce a concise written statement of vision and objectives that can be distributed throughout your organization.
- ☑ Have "stand-up meetings" to avoid too many lengthy discussions.
- ☑ Develop an in-house newsletter for weekly communication to the insiders.
- ☑ Manage by wandering around — stay in face-to-face contact with your key workers.
- ☑ As the leader, preach the vision to insiders as much as you do to outsiders.

**How to keep in touch with your followers.** Finally, a summary of principles discussed and suggested in this chapter, to help you avoid communication chaos:

1. Make internal communications a top priority of your job.
2. Keep your followers informed as to what you expect of them.
3. Finds ways to articulate and communicate vision and values.
4. Make sure that formal communication systems are in place.
5. Avoid the great surprise. If people are not doing their jobs well, tell them so.
6. Manage by wandering around.
7. Find ways to tap into the underground within your organization.
8. Practice HOT communication: Honest, Open, and Transparent. "Nothing happens until people talk."

# Missing the Clues
# of Corporate Culture
## *The Unseen Killer of Many a Leader*

▶ Corporate culture is "the way we do things around here."

▶ Never underestimate the mighty power of your organization's culture.

▶ Cultivating and changing the culture should be one of leadership's top priorities.

▶ Learn to respect values different from your own.

G et rid of those donuts and bring out the bran muffins!" I told my secretary after my first experience at a staff social event. "Haven't these people discovered the low-fat fitness revolution?"

"Take it easy, Hans—this is the Midwest, not California," she warned me.

Here was another example of corporate culture staring me in the face as I was getting adjusted to working in a new organizational setting in a new part of the country.

I have been intrigued to discover the concept of corporate culture over the last five years, and have made it a hobby to observe the cultures of organizations I come in contact with. And I have found that most Christians still don't know a lot about the concept.

Here are a few living illustrations of what corporate culture is all about:

> The boss calls in one of his new employees after several weeks on the job and says the following, "This corporation prides itself on being a friendly place to work, Matthews, and from now on we want you to be a heck of a lot friendlier."

A new woman working in a dentist's office is pulled aside by another employee and is reprimanded by her after several weeks on the job: "We dance the waltz around here. If you dance the polka, you won't make it."

A father, speaking to his son with pearls of wisdom as that son is about to enter the marketplace after graduation from college, shares with him the first rule of survival in a new job: "Find out how they keep score . . . and score."

I define corporate culture very simply as, "The way we do things around here." Or to make the definition a bit more formal: "An organization's corporate culture is the way insiders behave based on the values and group traditions they hold.

Take this quiz to see if you have ever bumped into corporate culture. Answer yes or no to the following questions:

> **Corporate Culture**
>
> **An organization's corporate culture is the way insiders behave based on the values and group traditions they hold.**

1. Are you a Macintosh or an IBM PC clone fanatic?
2. Do you change personality when you go see your in-laws? Does your spouse?
3. Have you felt the anxiety and surprise of moving into a new job situation?
4. Did you make any adjustments in your life when you got married?
5. Have you tried to reform and "reprogram" your spouse?
6. Have you experienced the changed dynamics and pressure of having to adjust to a new boss?
7. Do you find more *esprit de corps* and compatibility with certain kinds of people?

8. Have you ever felt you just don't fit the group you work with?
9. Have you had serious disagreements with other committed Christians who believe the same Bible you do?
10. Can you separate your theology from your methodology?
11. Do you ever feel that your coworkers just don't share your values?
12. Are you devoted to a particular airline? To a certain line of automobiles?
13. Are there certain groups or organizations you would not work for at any price?
14. If you were in charge, would you change your organization significantly?

If you answered yes to most of those questions, you have run into corporate culture! Organizational culture is like the glue in plywood—you are not totally aware of it until you try to take it apart!

I look at corporate culture the same way I look at human faces and personalities. Isn't it amazing that no two faces are alike, unless they are twins? With the billions of people on earth, God in His infinite creativity has designed every one of us with a different face, voice, fingerprint, and personality. Organizations are the same way. Each one has a totally unique and distinct personality, which we call its corporate culture. And that culture is built upon the values and belief systems that percolate up from the core of its leadership like molten lava bubbling out of a volcano.

Just what is *organizational culture?* And what, if anything, does it have to do with leadership? The term *culture* was for many years the domain of the anthropologist and sociologist. But today, it has become a buzzword in leadership and management circles. Anyone who has an interest in leadership or management will run into the concept of "corporate culture" on a regular basis. It is discussed broadly in a wide range of applications, and is increasingly recognized as one of the fundamental building blocks of organizational life.

Corporate culture is a powerful force. It can at times be so strong that people have a religious attitude toward their company, so devoted they are to its culture.

### Where Corporate Culture Shows Up

If you're married, you felt a strong dose of corporate culture when you realized that your spouse's family was not like your family. Each family, like each organization, has its own values that create a unique set of behavioral patterns.

Several years ago, while I was in graduate school in Dallas, I worked for several different companies over a short span of time. I recall so vividly the culture shock as I moved from one to the next. First I worked the night shift at a Fleischmann's margarine factory. That was my first exposure to died-in-the-wool union people. What a tight culture! I was nonunion, and they let me know it. That job lasted two weeks, then I left to work in sales for a security firm.

Now I was thrown into a fellowship of off-duty policemen. What a culture the law enforcement crowd is! They were worlds away from the Fleischmann crowd. About a year later I went to work in the construction and remodeling industry in North Dallas, fixing up grand old homes that were being revived. Again I found a distinct new subculture of people in the professional painters and carpenters.

If you've changed jobs from one organization to an-

| Where Culture Crops Up |
| --- |
| ✦ A new marriage |
| ✦ A new church |
| ✦ A new city |
| ✦ A new job |
| ✦ A new pastor |
| ✦ A new boss |
| ✦ A new generation |
| ✦ Conflict |
| ✦ Preferences |
| ✦ Tastes |
| ✦ Lifestyles |
| ✦ Ministry styles |

other, you felt corporate culture as you had to learn a new set of unwritten rules. When one walks into a new organization for the first time, one can feel the culture much more than an insider can. It has been observed that you cannot understand your own culture until you have traveled to another. The first time you visit another country for a few weeks, you begin to realize that the whole world does not think or act as we do in North America. And when you step off the plane back home, you see your own culture as never before. You get a small glimpse of what foreigners see when they first land on our shores.

Newcomers to organizations have the same feeling when they step "on the shore" of a new group. They feel that they have to learn "how to do things around here," and if they don't, fellow workers will let them know right away. Ralph Kilmann writes:

> The organization itself has an invisible quality—a certain style, a character, a way of doing things—that may be more powerful than the dictates of any one person or any formally documented system. To understand the essence or soul of the organization requires that we travel below the charts, rulebooks, machines, and buildings into the underground world of corporate cultures (*Beyond the Quick Fix*, 1984:92).

### Organizational Culture and Leadership

Just what is culture? It's a fuzzy term that means different things to different people. The dilemma of defining culture is highlighted by William B. Renner of the Aluminum Company of America:

> Culture is different things to different people. For some, it's family, or religion. It's opera or Shakespeare, a few clay pots at a Roman dig. Every textbook offers a definition, but I like a simple one: culture is the shared values and behavior that knit a community together.

It's the rules of the game; the unseen meaning between the lines in the rulebook that assures unity. All organizations have a culture of their own (Kilmann, 1984:92).

*Webster's New Collegiate Dictionary* defines culture as:

The integrated pattern of knowledge, belief and behavior that depends on man's capacity for learning and transmitting knowledge to succeeding generations. The customary beliefs, social forms, and material traits of a racial, religious, or social group.

Traditionally, culture has been defined as simply the unique *customs, values,* and *artifacts* of a people. Today there is a growing consensus that organizations have distinct cultures as well, the same distinct customs, values, and artifacts that we usually think of societies possessing. It is also a growing conviction in management circles that those cultures need to be understood, nurtured, and managed. If you miss the culture clues as a leader, you may be in for some tough times.

Companies like Intel and Avis are often cited as examples of companies that are successful because they devote much of their energies to the promotion and cultivation of corporate culture. They put much of their energy into managing employees' behavior though creating a strong culture.

In 1982, Thomas Peters and Robert Waterman wrote an immensely popular book, *In Search of Excellence: Lessons from America's Best-Run Companies,* in which they showed the benefits and characteristics of the strong corporate cultures of America's best-run organizations. Peters and Waterman brought to focus *a realization that strong cultures contribute to organizational success* when the culture supports the mission, goals, and strategy of the organization.

The pursuit of excellence is certainly something that anyone involved in leading a Christian organization ought to be about. The Scriptures exhort the church in numerous places to do whatever it does to *the glory of God*: "So whether you eat or drink or whatever you do, do it all for the glory of God" (1 Cor. 10:31). "And whatever you do, whether in word or deed, do it all in the name of the Lord Jesus, giving thanks to God the Father through Him" (Col. 3:17). A few verses later, Paul states, "Whatever you do, work at it with all your heart, as working for the Lord, not for men, since you know that you will receive an inheritance from the Lord as a reward. It is the Lord Christ you are serving" (Col. 3:23-24).

### The Human Side of Christian Organizations

A number of years ago I was beginning my first full-time ministry in a local church in Southern California. At the same time that I was in the church as the pastor, Donna was working for a company called Oilwell. As we compared notes many evenings about our days at the office, I was amazed that there was a more supportive community and more care for the workers in her company than in our church. That was when I first realized that for many Christians it is more fulfilling and enjoyable to work in well-run secular organizations than in the poorly organized, stressful environments of many Christian organizations. To put it even more simply, it is often a whole lot more fun to work in the world than in the church. Why? Because the church is behind on understanding basic principles of how humans work well together.

If we devote more attention to the details of shaping the organizations God has appointed us to lead, then the people whom He calls to work within them will indeed find long-term productivity and fruitfulness in a fulfilling environment. Jesus knew that nonbelievers often make wiser leaders than the sons of the kingdom:

> The master commended the dishonest manager because he had acted shrewdly. For the people of this

world are more shrewd in dealing with their own kind than are the people of light (Luke 16:8).

It was the steward's astuteness, not his morality which was commended. One commentator rewrites the passage like this: "The children of this world look further ahead, in dealing with their own generation, than the children of light" (Morris, 1974:248). Anyone who has worked in a Christian organization very long knows that each Christian group has its own way of doing things. Whether secular or sacred, organizations have cultures and each is unique. And these ways of doing things are passed down from founders to their heirs, generation after generation.

### So How Do We Find Our Corporate Culture?
The obvious question at this point is: How do I know what our organization's culture is? One way to answer that question would be to take some time to sit down with your leadership group and describe your corporate culture. I would suggest using two categories, making a distinction between your organization's values and beliefs, values which I would call "preferences," and beliefs, which I would define as "moral absolutes."

| Contrasting Values & Beliefs in Corporate Culture | |
| --- | --- |
| **Values** | **Beliefs** |
| Preferences | Moral absolutes |
| Tastes | Black and white |
| Regional & cultural | Ethical issues |
| Methodology, not | Right and |
| theology | wrong values |

Here are some samples of values and beliefs. As you read the list, answer these questions: Which of these values or beliefs would I fight over? Which of these would I quit over?

Which are nonnegotiable? Which do I disagree with? Put a plus in the margin by the values and beliefs that you agree with. Put a minus by the ones that you are neutral on, and strike out the ones that you strongly oppose. When you're done, ask yourself this final question: "How many of my colleagues would answer as I have?"

### Values: preferences, tastes.
- We will use the latest technology to do our work.
- More technology is better than less.
- Time is more valuable than money.
- The reduction of paperwork is important.
- We won't do it if it's not quality.
- Anything important will be written in a report.
- Speed is of the essence.
- Precision is of the essence.
- Better to get it done right than to fail because it was not perfect.
- Our people must learn the languages in the countries where we work.
- We will submit to the cultures of the other lands in which we work.

### Beliefs: moral absolutes, black-and-white issues.
- We will have open, honest relationships and ask forgiveness if we wrong another worker in our organization.
- Theft will not be tolerated among our people.
- My children come before my work.
- Lying can have no place between our workers.
- We will not hold bitternesses.
- We cannot tolerate immorality among our workers.
- Planting new churches is the best way to fulfill the Great Commission.
- We must show compassion to the poor and suffering.
- The Bible is God's inerrant inspired revelation to mankind.
- Our workers must reflect ethnic diversity.

If you compare notes with a colleague on your responses to that list, you may find that you disagree even about which list a particular item should be on. What one person thinks is a *value* another may view as a *belief*—an absolute. I know Macintosh owners who are convinced that it's morally responsible to be loyal to Apple! To some people the world is black and white, and everything is a moral issue. Such people are hard to work with and hard to work for. They are inflexible and tend to think that their way is the only way.

Understanding the difference between values and beliefs has been a very liberating thing for me. Some issues simply are not worth fighting over. Many times we have to respect the right of others to have a different set of values than we have.

As a leader, spend some time alone and sort out your own values and beliefs. Then work it through with your leadership team and come up with a list of the values and beliefs your whole team stands for. This list becomes the powerful glue that holds you together, like the individual layers in a sheet of plywood.

Secular companies know this principle well. One of the most successful mail order companies in America is Land's End, based in Wisconsin. These premier direct-mail merchants have boiled down their culture into four clearly articulated corporate values. These four pillars of the company determine their daily actions in organizational life:

### Land's End

1. Make your merchandise as good as you can.
2. Always, always price it fairly.
3. Make it a snap to shop for, twenty-four hours a day.
4. Guarantee it, period.

Sun Valley Waterbeds, based on the West Coast, has become one of America's top providers of a good night's sleep. They know what they are after and have articulated it well in their communications—first with their employees and then to their customers:

**Sun Valley Waterbeds**
"Our Precepts"
We believe that we sincerely provide a better night's sleep.
We believe our products are of a proven high quality at a fair price, representing the best possible value.
We believe in serving customers in such a manner as to earn their continuing respect, confidence, trust, and support, both before and after the sale.
We believe we should treat our customers, dealers, suppliers, and employees with human dignity and integrity, observing the highest moral and ethical standards in all aspects of our business.
We believe the customer is always right.
We believe in being a good corporate citizen by contributing to the economic and social well-being of every community in which we operate.
We believe in being the most respected company in the industry.

> **Corporate Value Statements Are:**
>
> *Like Glue*
> They help leaders hold an organization together.
>
> *Like a Magnet*
> They attract newcomers as members, employees, customers, or donors.
>
> *A Ruler*
> By which a leader can measure how his or her group is doing.

Finally, an example from a local church that has taken the same principle and clearly articulated its core values in a simple-to-remember format. Rick Warren, the highly effective pastor of Saddleback Community Church in Orange County, California, spells out to his church and to the public at large the values that guide the church:

## THE SADDLEBACK STRATEGY

**S** Simple structure: we emphasize relationships.

**A** Acceptance: we offer friendliness and openness.

**D** Defined purpose: we exist for four distinct reasons — to celebrate God's presence, communicate His Word, educate His people, and demonstrate His love.

**D** Defined target: to respond to the hurts, needs, and interests of our community.

**L** Lay ministry: our church runs by lay ministries.

**E** Encouraging preaching: our preaching emphasizes personal, practical solutions from God's Word for life's common problems.

**B** Build up before building out: we build people before buildings.

**A** Advertising: we do so to share our church with the community.

**C** Contemporary worship: a style that is culturally relevant.

**K** Keep on growing: because everybody needs what Christ offers.

### The Value of Understanding Corporate Culture

There are many reasons why "culture audits" are valuable for Christian organizations. They can help leaders understand the underlying dynamics that drive their organization. Beliefs and values that are circulating deep beneath the surface can be identified, discussed, and evaluated. More specifically, here are some of the ways your organization can benefit from understanding its own corporate culture:

*Evaluation of Christian values and beliefs.* For the Christian organization, whether a mission agency, a parachurch group, a church, or a church-related group, there should be distinctives that make it different from secular institutions in the way it operates. The Christian should hold viewpoints rooted in biblical Christianity that differ noticeably from a secular worldview. In reality, what an organization espouses as its Christian values and beliefs often differs dramatically from its actual practices. For example, the group can say that it values family life but then demand so much from its leaders that their families are ruined in the process. Any Christian organization must ask itself if it is truly practicing what it upholds as the necessary standards for Christian ministry.

*Organizational effectiveness.* Many writers in the field of organizational culture point to the issue of group effectiveness as one of the most far-reaching benefits of understanding corporate culture. The culture of an organization can work for or against the goals of the group.

Major problems can arise in a group that has developed values or beliefs in conflict with the actual mission of the group. As an example, I know of a ministry that has

| **Applications: Corporate Culture in the Nitty-gritty** |
| --- |
| ◆ **Discerning guidance** |
| ◆ **Making new friends** |
| ◆ **Finding a life partner** |
| ◆ **Finding a church home** |
| ◆ **Looking for a new job** |
| ◆ **Conflict management** |
| ◆ **Recruitment & placement** |
| ◆ **Management** |
| ◆ **Staff training** |
| ◆ **Organizational effectiveness** |
| ◆ **Advertising & promotion** |
| ◆ **Bringing about change** |
| ◆ **Visionary leadership: tending the culture** |

as its goal to be innovative and contemporary in evangelizing America's youth culture. Yet the organization is burdened down with a stifling paper bureaucracy that lives in the past and is slow to change. They have a future-oriented ministry purpose, tied to a culture rooted in tradition, looking at the past.

Groups can take on goals that are incompatible with the underlying assumptions of the organization. To understand the culture of the organization is to know what the organization will be good at doing, and what it should avoid.

***Understanding division and strife.*** There are actually different subcultures within any organization. At times two subcultures can become so incompatible that there will be a split, an event that often happens in local church settings. I have witnessed not a few churches fighting over forms of worship and music, with different subcultures believing that their way is the right way.

A large Christian organization which ministers to children recently had a major rift that came to the surface after several years of tension. A large subculture within the organization, including some of the top leadership, left to begin a new work with identical goals. The group that departed had become so uncomfortable in the "host culture," that they felt their only option was disassociation. Basic assumptions

---

Leaders who understand their own values and can articulate them well to the organization have proven to show superior performance in their roles. In *The Leadership Challenge*, James Kouzes and Barry Posner list six significant payoffs for both managers and their organizations when the leaders were able to articulate a unified, distinct organizational culture. Understanding your organization's culture:

1. Fosters strong feelings of personal effectiveness.
2. Promotes high levels of company loyalty.
3. Facilitates consensus about key organizational goals.
4. Encourages ethical behavior.
5. Reduces levels of job stress and tension.
6. Promotes strong norms about working hard and caring.

*—Kouzes and Posner,*
The Leadership Challenge,
*1988:193*

and beliefs in the two subcultures had become incompatible.

A culture audit can bring to the surface conflicts that are deep within the organization and which are stifling all possibilities for effectiveness.

***Leadership compatibility.*** In the case just described, one subculture felt incompatible with another. There are also times when a leader is incompatible with the culture of the group. This is often the case when a pulpit committee recruits a new pastor without doing the necessary "culture homework." The basic assumptions of the prospective new leader should be compared with the basic assumptions of the organization—point by point—for cultural compatibility. Such a comparison can easily be done during the recruitment stage. The search committee should look at how the potential pastor or leader looks at various issues that the host group holds dear. Unfortunately, there is usually much more emphasis on infatuation and subjective feelings than there is deep discussion about values and beliefs.

I recently watched just such a recruitment effort go up in smoke. A strong leader was recruited for a church that held plurality of leadership as its basic approach to management. The leader felt he was in charge, but the group of leaders who recruited him felt he would be only one among equals, and that all decisions would be made in the group, by consensus. Needless to say, conflicts soon arose.

Another problem in that mismatch was that the leader was from a blue-collar background and had only pastored blue-collar congregations. His new church was a high-tech "yuppie" church that was initially wowed by his preaching but soon found that nothing he said was connecting with them. Leaders must be a good cultural fit for the organization in order to enjoy a long tenure of effective service.

***Leadership behavior.*** Christian leaders should act differently than those in the secular world. They should treat their workers differently, they should view their mission in a different light, and they should be driven by different motivations. Since the leader is the keeper of the culture, it falls on his or her shoulders to cultivate a culture that is distinctly Christian. The values and beliefs that leader holds usually become the assumptions of the followers. That puts a great deal of responsibility on the shoulders of leadership.

Christian leaders should strive to live a model of servant leadership that is distinct from the secular corporate executive in basic areas. A mission CEO recently resigned overnight to take a new position with another organization. The shock of his resignation was damaging to the organization, because they had made so many changes in ministry strategy *at his request.* After only a few years in the CEO position, and after making many deep changes in the mission, the leader simply walked away with no warning. When asked by the chairman of the board why he did not share his desire to move on or discuss the move with anyone, the former CEO replied, "Well, that's the way they do it in the corporate world; it's all very secret." In the body of Christ things ought to be different, because we view our work and our relationships with one another in a different light.

*"Followership" issues.* In Christian work, members of the organization have a God-given responsibility to care for one another as members of the body of Christ. The Scriptures that delineate the actions as a community in Christ should apply to all Christian organizations, creating a way of relating different from that of secular society. The employees, staff, or missionaries of a Christian organization are equals in Christ, and are to be respected, loved, and cared for in Christian commitment. The Christian organization must look at this area and make sure that their model for follower care is built on Scripture, not on a corporate model of use and abuse.

On the other side, followers are to respect and honor the leaders God has placed over them as unto the Lord (1 Thes.

5:12-13). Disrespect for authority should not be tolerated in a Christian corporate culture.

***Placement issues in recruitment and personnel.*** Equally as important as the fit of the leader with the organizational culture is the fit of the followers. When an organization is recruiting workers, it must be careful to choose people who are culturally compatible, and must be honest with potential recruits about the corporate culture they are being recruited to join.

When I am out recruiting for our organization, I know exactly what we value and stand for. The more I can communicate that clearly, the more potential recruits will get an honest appraisal of what it would be like to work for us. Too many people are promised one thing only to discover an entirely different world when they go to work for the new outfit.

***Staff training.*** I can think of no better way to orient new staff to your group than to take them point-by-point through your list of values and beliefs. By so doing you are (a) teaching them what you believe, (b) explaining to them why you emphasize what you emphasize, and (c) indoctrinating them into the very soul and belief system of the organization.

***Discerning the will of God in career guidance.*** The issue of discerning the will of God in one's career is the other side of the coin of recruitment. When one is looking for a group to join, an organization to work for, or a church to pastor, it is imperative that the person doing the searching investigate the basic cultural values of the group and compare those with his or her own.

There are many types of Christian organizations and denominations, with vastly different values and beliefs. Instead of walking into a situation where there is a poor cultural fit, it would be best for the person doing the seeking to try to work with a group that, as closely as possible, shares his or her values and beliefs.

***Issues of mergers, acquisitions, or joint efforts.*** There are times when Christian groups, like secular corporations, find it helpful to merge, acquire, or work jointly with other groups. Several years ago I attended a church that merged with another assembly of equal size. The experiment was successful because the elders talked through very specifically the issues of corporate values of both groups, and worked hard at the top to honor and blend those value systems into one. And the groups were quite compatible, though not identical to begin with.

In many overseas mission situations, different organizations work together in cooperative efforts, and at times one mission will actually merge with another. In all of these situations it is helpful to ask questions about cultural compatibility before the groups come together. One can anticipate problems that will arise — and they usually do — if one can see the difference in assumptions between the groups.

One mission, for example, began to work with another that had strong differences with them in their views regarding time, resources, and relationships. Mission A held that communication should be formal and through written memos and correspondence. Relationships were primarily official and through clear lines of administrative channels, systems, and paperwork. Mission B, in contrast, valued networking and informal, open lines of communication, and did not use paper to communicate. If one person at Mission B needed to get a message to another, the telephone was the tool of choice, regardless of long-distance costs. At Mission A, no one used the phone to communicate. As the two groups began to work together, Mission B angered the leaders at Mission A with their constant, interrupting, "wasteful" phone calls, while Mission B was annoyed at the unresponsiveness over at Mission A, and ignored their "bureaucratic" flood of paperwork. To this day the two groups have not learned to communicate — because of their radically different organizational cultures.

***Visionary leadership and change.*** One of the core jobs of a leader is to be the "tender of the culture," the person who nurtures and develops the group's understanding of itself. The more he or she knows about the group's existing culture, the easier it will be to lead and to promote needed change.

## To Fit or Not to Fit: Cultural Harmony and Dissonance

All of the issues just explored have one thing in common: they deal with issues of cultural "fit." Cultural fit can be viewed in terms of harmony and dissonance. Understanding the unique organizational culture of a group of people helps one understand who fits with that group and who does not. Whether dealing with followers or leaders, new employees or old, there are people who fit in organizations and others who don't. At times the lack of fit is in areas of beliefs, where moral issues of right and wrong are at stake.

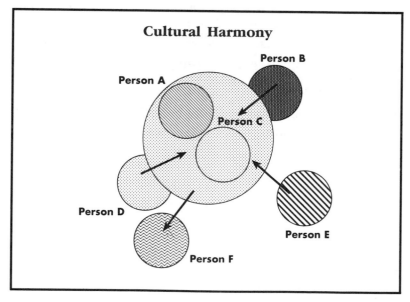

Other times it is in value areas, where one person strongly feels a preference for doing things in a way that is not the common practice of the group.

These important issues of harmony and dissonance can be seen in the following "Cultural Harmony" illustration, using circles to represent different people and the big circle to represent your organization with its corporate culture.

The big circle is your organization, with its unique culture. Person A is working for you, but doesn't really fit or feel "at home." (More in a moment on what happens to people like him.) Persons B and E are unlike A, and are on their way into the group from the outside. They are new employees/members who will either change to conform to the group, or become like Person A, not feeling at home. Persons C and D are ideal, for they completely share the values and beliefs of the group. You need lots of Cs and Ds, but don't forget that the absence of some mavericks will eventually spell institutionalized boredom! Don't drive away all the Fs, because they think differently.

The more a person buys into the corporate value and belief system of an organization, the more cultural harmony there will be between that person and the group. And of course, conversely, the more differences there are, the more one finds dissonance within the group.

**Cultural Adaptation, or, Who Stays and Who Leaves?**
Dealing with these issues of cultural harmony and dissonance leads to the important issue of cultural adaptation. Not everyone within an organization has totally committed themselves to the organizational culture, the values and beliefs of the core group. Especially for newcomers, it may take months to uncover the core and learn what the people really believe. When there is dissonance with the group's beliefs and values, these newcomers will either:

1. Adapt wholeheartedly and promote the culture enthusiastically.

2. Adapt reluctantly and submit to the culture passively.
3. Reject the culture and try to change it.
4. Reject the culture and be a troublemaker, while remaining miserable.
5. Reject the culture and leave.
6. Reject the culture and make everyone miserable trying to change it.

Are these issues of culture fit applicable to Christian organizations? If we hold to the standards of biblical Christianity, don't we all believe the same way? The answer is a resounding no! Christians differ dramatically in both beliefs and values, and can best serve their Master if they yoke themselves with Christians in the body of Christ who see things in roughly the same way as they do. I believe God created many different kinds of Christians to reach many different kinds of people. Use the principle of "different strokes for different folks," and join with a group you find culturally compatible. If you are a leader, lead those who, as closely as possible, value and believe what you do.

At times, I suspect, God places individuals into organizations where they don't fit

---

### Six Reactions to Culture Conflict

**Conformer**
"I've just got to accept things the way they are."

**Complainer**
"I may have to work here, but I don't have to like it."

**Innovator**
"Let's change things around here!"

**Ritualist**
"Job? What job? I'm just going through the motions."

**Retreatist**
"I've got to get out of this situation ASAP!"

**Rebel**
"They can't make me conform —I'll show them!"

---

for a reason, either to teach the organization things it needs to learn, or to work on the development of the person who is the poor fit.

## POWERPOINTS

By way of application, let's look first at four concrete points to get your group thinking about corporate culture. Then, a biblical model of how to respond to the different cultures in your organization:

### How to Harness Your Corporate Culture

☑ *Put your own culture down on paper:* Take the time to write down your values and beliefs. Use one page for each. After you've written them down, share them with your leaders and see how yours and theirs match up.

☑ *Come up with your group's list of corporate values:* Try to move from the views of the individuals to that which the group as a whole holds as most important. When you complete this process you will have a list of the basic core values of your organization.

☑ *Develop a vision statement for your group:* Develop a vision statement that reflects where you are going as a group. Make sure that all your top leaders are a part of writing this statement and that they can sign off on it "in blood."

☑ *Communicate your culture clearly to insiders and outsiders:* When the culture is identified and the mission clearly stated, preach it from the housetops both to insiders and to your constituents or customers.

### THE BIBLICAL MODEL: SENSITIVITY

Here are a few foundational principles for dealing with differences in values and beliefs:

***Listen to win:*** Develop the ability to listen to others who may not agree with you (see 1 Cor. 9:19-23).

***Love diversity:*** Recognize that the body of Christ, His church, is made up of many different gifts and contributions. It would be a boring family of faith if we were all alike (see Eph. 4:1-17).

***Look for unity:*** Even if you have differences, celebrate your unity on the fundamentals amid the diversity of various value systems among God's children. You are all one in the body of Christ (see Gal. 3:26-29).

***Learn to like those who are different:*** We are admonished in Scripture to "accept one another" in love. The Apostle Peter was rebuked for his bad attitude toward those who were unlike him. Learn to love and emotionally accept those who differ from you (see Acts 10:9-38).

***Learn to separate methodology from theology:*** Draw your lines in the sand where it counts, but don't make value differences moral issues. Hold to your theology passionately, but don't force your amoral preferences for doing ministry on everyone else. Different men and women will develop different ways of doing work, but don't let those personalities become divisive (see 1 Cor. 3:1-9).

***Long for His glory:*** The burden on the heart of Christ during His prayer before the Crucifixion was that we His church would be one. Whether or not we see things alike on the fine points, He is glorified when we walk in unity (see John 17:1-5, 20-23).

# Success without Successors
## *Planning Your Departure the Day You Begin*

▶ Pride tightens the grip on leadership;
humility relaxes and lets go.

▶ Finishing well is an important measure
of success in leadership.

▶ Letting go of leadership is like sending your children
away to college: It hurts, but has to be done.

▶ Mentoring is a nonnegotiable function
of successful leadership.

There I was, right in the middle of trench warfare between the old guy and his new successor. What a rude awakening to the terrors that some leadership transitions take on!

Right out of graduate school I joined the staff of a large church in Southern California. The pastor who hired me was new himself, having just taken over for the former pastor, who had been at the helm for twenty-six years. It's hard for anyone to follow such a long tenure of leadership. But what set this situation up for disaster was the crazy decision of the church trustees to allow the old pastor to stay on the pastoral team for a prolonged two-year transition.

Here was the ill-fated plan that the trustees and the tenured pastor hatched: They thought to themselves, "Since our leader has been so wonderful for so many years, who can possibly replace him and run our beloved institution?" (This was a declining and graying congregation, that had grown up with the pastor.) So they decided to look for a new pastor, who during his first year would be mentored by the old pastor. The plan was that during the second year the two would switch roles, with the older man becoming assistant to the new man. After two years the old guy would ride off into the sunset and the church would boldly face the future in peace and harmony.

What's wrong with this picture? Nothing, if we lived in a perfect world. It failed to take into account two major issues: the pride of leadership, and the depravity of man. Soon after the new, younger man (who, by the way, was in his fifties) arrived, he began to generate a following among the younger and more aggressive people in the church who wanted change. And the older man, with the old guard, began to feel threatened. Soon the old pastor let it be known that he was not pleased with the "new directions" being taken by his new associate.

The shoe finally dropped during the final weeks of that hot August, and the old pastor resigned in protest of the directions of his successor. Fast-forwarding to the ultimate outcome, the church developed a vicious division into two camps—"I follow the old" versus "I side with the new"—and the new pastor was voted out of the church. The church was left leaderless and deeply divided. Fifteen years later, it has never recovered from the immaturity and damage of that failed leadership transition. Though the older pastor had spent many fruitful years of leadership in that situation, he did not finish well as he ruined his successor's chances for success.

> ## Leadership Transitions
>
> Of all the leadership transition mistakes, two occur most frequently:
>
> ◆ Leaders tend to stay too long in a position rather than not long enough.
>
> ◆ Leaders who stay too long do much more damage than those who don't stay long enough.
>
> —*Lyle Schaller*

In vivid contrast, as different as the midnight sky is to high noon, I found myself again in the middle of a major leadership transition recently. This one worked with textbook orderliness. In this case, the older man—leader for twenty-two years—turned over the reins and walked away in gracious humility.

He handed those reins to me.

When I recently became executive director of our fifty-year-old organization, I was part of an amazingly orderly leadership transition. CBFMS, like so many organizations across this land, is just at the tail end of what I call the "generational changing of the guard." My predecessor, Dr. Webster, finished well by focusing on the future even though he knew he would not be a part of it.

While I was in the process of being screened for appointment, I recall vividly one statement Dr. Webster made to me: "Success without a successor is failure." He honestly believes this principle, and lived it out by allowing for a smooth and orderly transfer of power.

How many leaders at that place in life make things ugly by not leaving when they should, or by undermining the new leader? In contrast, Dr. Webster affirmed me, supported me, mentored me, and launched me into my new role with great fanfare. And he knew that I was as different from him as night is from day in my leadership style. It was obvious to him—and he communicated this to the board of directors and senior staff—that our organization was in need of change. Upon his departure I told him, "I hope, when it comes my turn to hand the reins to the next person, that I will have half of the graciousness and humility that you have had."

## The Ongoing Successor Search

Success without a successor is failure. Who are the men and women you are grooming to one day take your place? I keep a running list in my Daytimer of the up-and-coming leaders who may someday down the road be ready to pick up where I leave off. I look them over and think, *Yes, he could become director of this. She will be ready for that role in a few years.* In fact, sometimes as I speak to our younger staff, I look into their faces and think, *One of you will replace me someday!* That thought excites me and motivates me to pave the way for them. They are not a threat, but the ultimate completion of my leadership.

Organizations live and die on the basis of their flow of new leadership talent. As we saw when considering corporate life cycles, the only way to guarantee that your group does not slide down the back side of the curve to institutionalization, calcification, and death is to constantly renew yourself with fresh blood in the form of new leaders.

One of my priorities as a leader is the mentoring of our emerging leadership pool. I'm in my forties, and they are in their early thirties and even twenties. But I will watch them and help them and nurture them whenever I can. As often as possible, I ask myself, *Who are your men?* Who are the people I am targeting and developing for future leadership? This is not playing favorites, it is preparing for the future.

Every one of the more than 850 people who work somewhere in our global organization warrants my attention as his or her leader. But I cannot be close to everyone, and must therefore work primarily through the senior staff who surround me at our headquarters. I keep one eye trained on leading my present leaders, and the other on the rising pool of new talent. The eye that is trained on the new talent looks through the viewfinder of a rifle, not a shotgun. I cannot develop everyone to lead at the highest levels, because many follow and few lead. Without showing favoritism, I attempt to focus in on the few rising stars who seem to show greatest promise.

I watch these men and women, and try to encourage their advancement through growing levels of responsibility and leadership. I listen to what others say about them—an informal but very effective way to get "references"! And of course I take careful note of two important traits of successful leaders: how well they get along with *people,* and how good they are at *getting excellent work accomplished.* This is nothing more than the sound principle Jesus spoke of two millennia ago:

His master replied, "Well done, good and faithful servant! You have been faithful with a few things; I will
put you in charge of many things. Come and share
your master's happiness!" (Matt. 25:21)

At a recent executive retreat I led my nine associates
through an interesting value-sharing exercise to drive home
the issue of mentoring our emerging leadership pool. My
desire was to get them to think in terms of the small group
of men and women each of them is developing for future
leadership. I asked them to imagine that we were ship-
wrecked on an island with only a radio and eighteen minutes of battery life left, at best. Each of us have two minutes
to share with the home office what is most important to
remember in case we never make it back. And included in
that two-minute broadcast must be instructions about whom
we are appointing to carry on for us should we not return.

This exercise forced two important issues: What do you
value most, and whom do you trust most to carry on for
you? It was a very lively and revealing discussion. Each of us
went away renewed in our desire to mentor a select few of
our up-and-coming leaders.

### Barriers to Successful Successors
There are as many unsuccessful leadership transitions as
there are successful ones. I imagine that everyone reading
this book has witnessed firsthand a leadership transfer that
went wrong. The reasons for such fiascos vary, but most
often include one or more of the following:

- The organization just doesn't like the new person.
- The new person just doesn't like the organization.
- There is a corporate culture conflict: Values and beliefs don't match.
- The leader fails miserably in his newly assigned responsibilities: He lacks either the ability, capacity,
  experience, or knowledge to do the job.

- The old guard sabotages the efforts of the new leader.
- The old leader sabotages the efforts of the new leader.
- The old leader fails to leave, or reappears.
- The new leader lacks persistence to implement change.
- The new leader is recruited away by a better offer or challenge.
- The new leader fails to win a following because of poor interpersonal skills.

I have a close friend on the West Coast who has become the general manager of business owned by his wife's family. He has worked for his father-in-law for many years, and took over the role of general manager and CEO about five years ago. The transition has been and continues to be a painful one. It seems that family businesses and organizations that are led by founder/CEOs, have the worst track record with leadership transitions.

My friend's father-in-law built this successful business with his bare hands—through hardships, the Depression, and decades of sweat and toil. His son-in-law can't seem to do anything right, and dear old Dad never lets him forget it. About a year ago the in-laws moved to another city, just to get away from the situation, supposedly to give the son-in-law some room to breathe. But even from that remote site his father-in-law sows seeds of discord and pessimism through his continued connections to the family and some of the workers in the business. And since Mom- and Dad-in-law are still the major shareholders, their power does not wane.

What is this man's problem? He simply cannot ride off into the sunset, even though he is retired. He cannot let go of something that is so personal to him. To its founders, a family business is a child. You never let go of your emotional attachment to your children. No one can parent the firm the way he did it, so my poor friend can't win. He continually suffers from high blood pressure that goes up and down directly in proportion to his father-in-law's association with the company.

### Why Leader's Can't Let Go

The previous list gave some of the general reasons why the leadership succession system breaks down, and why some new leaders don't last very long. Now let's look at the issue from the perspective of the retiring leader, who needs to make way for his or her successor. The reasons for not letting go of leadership are powerful ones:

*Job security.* What will I do and where will I go next? Besides, I'm enjoying my work, so why should I think of leaving? And who wants a leader my age? The open slots are being filled by the younger generations.

A leader who is a true servant of the organization will put the group's needs before his or her own.

*Fear of retirement.* This closely parallels the issue of job security, and of course remains for many the ultimate fear—the fear of eventual uselessness. It is a proven fact that this fear is much greater in men than in women, for they tend to find more of their self-worth from their work.

---

**Barriers to Grooming Your Successor**

*Job security*
What am I going to do next?

*Fear of retirement*
Me, retire?

*Resistance to change*
The saddle is so comfortable.

*Self-worth*
This role is my whole life

*Lack of confidence*
Who else can do this job like I do?

*Love for the job*
I really love my leadership role

*Loss of investment*
I've put too much into this group to let it go

***Resistance to change.*** We get comfortable with familiar surroundings and regular routines (a rut is a grave with the ends knocked out!) and resist drastic change in our lives. "How can I possibly shift to another organization? It would inconvenience my family to uproot them. It's much easier to stay where I am than to go through the traumatic upheaval of a major geographic and social relocation."

***Self-worth.*** The normal adult (especially male) gains the greatest portion of his or her identity from his job. To tamper with my job is to destroy my identity. For many a leader, her job is the very essence of his or her self-worth. To lose that role of leadership is to lose all confidence and identity. This is especially true of workaholics.

***Lack of confidence in a successor.*** We lack confidence that anyone else will do as good a job as we can do. We can always see reasons to stay another year or season—or another decade—to make sure that things get taken care of "properly," that is, *our* way.

***Love for the people and the job.*** This is perhaps the most emotional of all the reasons for hanging on to our jobs. We love our work and we don't want to leave it. Why leave the warmth of our role and organization for the cold realities of a new, alien environment? Why retire to boredom and loneliness when I can hang on with the people I love to be with?

***Loss of investment.*** CEOs, senior pastors, and founders place huge amounts of personal effort into building their corporations. It is an investment that is hard to let go of, much like letting go of children when they leave the nest.

These are all real concerns, yet they do not justify our permanence. Let me speak more candidly about that sixth reason—our love for the people and the job.

### The Pain of Parting

As we tooled down the backroads of what was then East Germany, I couldn't believe we both felt the same way. Somewhere between Dresden and Herrenhut (home of Count Zinzendorf) the tears began to well up in both of our eyes as we awkwardly said our good-byes. We simultaneously realized that it would not be in the future as it had been these last couple of years. We enjoyed being together. Our work in East Germany was going great. Saying good-bye for good was painful and we wanted to avoid it. Yet it was our choice to go our separate ways.

I had been the country director of our work in East Germany for several years. We had witnessed the joy of seeing a group of East Germans grow in their leadership ability. Now it was time to say good-bye and turn the work over to them. As Werner and I rode down the country roads speaking my native German, my mind flashed years ahead to the day when I will have to send the first of my four children away to college. *I bet it will feel just like this,* I thought. It's the right thing to do, but oh, so painful to part our ways. It will be painful because it will be permanent. Never again will my children come to live in our home like they did as children, and never again will Werner and I work side-by-side in this ministry in his land.

Leaving East Germany was the right thing for me to do, but it hurt. Had we not said good-bye, we would still be "running the show" and they would not have geared up to take over. Until we got out of the way, they were content to let us lead, though deep down inside they wanted to take a stab at it themselves. Now we have been gone for three years, and they are doing great without us. Does that make me feel insecure? Never! It's all a part of leadership working itself out of a job.

The Apostle Paul spent more time with the Christians at Ephesus than with any other group, but he did leave them eventually. Why? I'm sure they offered him a permanent faculty position and nice housing. He left because there was work for him to do in other places. He trained leaders and then cut them loose, with the freedom to build the work in their area. It was a good thing that Paul departed; can you imagine leading in his shadow?

Yet, listen to the pain of his departure:

When he had said this, he knelt down with all of them and prayed. They all wept as they embraced him and kissed him. What grieved them most was his statement that they would never see his face again (Acts 20:36-38).

### Mentoring: The Succession Process

So how is the process of developing our successors really carried out? It is a process that has much to do with mentoring. Paul Stanley and Robert Clinton, in their book *Connecting* (© 1992 by Stanley and Clinton. Used by permission of NavPress, Colorado Springs, CO. All rights reserved. For copies call 1-800-366-7788.) have developed a

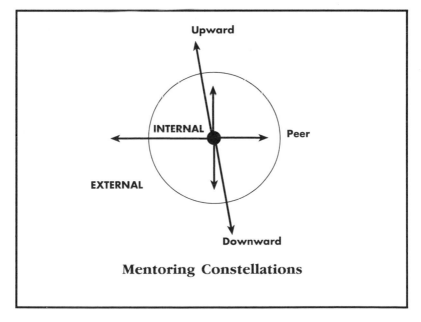

**Mentoring Constellations**

model of mentoring which they call the "constellation model." They define mentoring as, "a relational experience in which one person empowers another by sharing God-given resources."

The idea behind the constellation approach to mentoring is that a leader needs all different kinds of mentoring relationships to succeed in his or her leadership. Mentoring includes upward, downward, external, and internal relationships. I describe them as follows, including an example of one of my own mentors in each category:

**Upward mentoring.** First, there are the leaders who have gone before us, to whom we look up. They hold us accountable and stretch us. We are the leaders who will eventually succeed them.

*Example:* Do you remember Arno from the chapter on mavericks? Though he has left our organization, he is to this day an important upward mentor. I often look to him to test my ideas.

Probably the biggest upward mentor in my life is my father-in-law, Mark Bubeck. This chapter concludes with a poem he wrote this summer about "passing the torch."

**Downward mentoring.** Then, there are the people who will one day replace *us* in our leadership role. They are the "rifle vision" small group of people we are always thinking about developing into leaders. Some of them are in our own organization; others are outsiders.

Example: I first met Andreas in Vienna in 1982. He was a young man right out of graduate school and very confused about his future. We became good friends and he began to view me as his chief mentor—really as the big brother he never had. Over a decade has gone by and we are still good friends and he still looks to me for guidance and advice. He went on to earn a Ph.D. at Trinity Seminary in Illinois. Today he is a New Testament and Greek professor in Canada. I am grateful for having had the opportunity to help him find himself and a fulfilling career.

***Internal peer mentoring.*** Then there are peers within our organization who challenge us to do better, and who hold us accountable in our personal lives and leadership responsibilities.

Example: Last summer we hired Mike to move from Portland and join us at our headquarters in Chicagoland. He has become a trusted friend and personal challenge. Mike prays for me and asks me the kind of probing personal questions someone needs to ask. We go jogging at lunchtime two or three days a week—a time I look forward to because he is going to challenge me spiritually and physically.

***External peer mentoring.*** There are also peer co-mentoring relationships of individuals who are roughly at our stage of maturity and career advancement, who are outside our organization. Here is where the power of networking comes to play in the mentoring process.

Example: Sam and I are both directors of similar organizations. And we are both baby boomers with very similar corporate values. I love getting together with Sam whenever possible, for he challenges and probes and stimulates my thinking on the long-range, strategic planning level. As an outsider, he can say things to me that insiders are afraid to tell their boss. When he criticizes or questions corporate practices and strategies, I listen carefully. For he has nothing at stake except our friendship and his desire to see me do my best.

I am encouraged by the new emphasis on mentoring in the last few years. In Stanley and Clinton's research on leaders who made a difference over a lifetime, they found that without exception these leaders had identified *three to ten people who had made significant contributions to their development.* And in studying major biblical figures and the biographies of great Christian leaders, they also came to the conclusion that one of the influences most often used by God to develop leaders was a *person or persons who had something to share that the leader needed.*

What makes a good mentor? According to Stanley and Clinton, people who influence the next generation of leaders have these common characteristics:

◆ The ability to readily see potential in a person
◆ Tolerance of mistakes, brashness, abrasiveness, and the like in order to see that potential develop
◆ Flexibility in responding to people in circumstances
◆ Patience: knowing that time and experience are needed for development
◆ Perspective: having vision and ability to see down the road, and to suggest the next steps a mentoree needs to take
◆ Gifts and abilities that build up and encourage others

And how exactly do mentors do their job of mentoring? Again, Stanley and Clinton have identified five important specifics:

◆ Mentors give to mentorees:
  a. Timely advice
  b. Letters, articles, books, or other literary information that offers perspectives
  c. Finances
  d. Freedom to emerge as a leader even beyond the level of the mentor

◆ Mentors risk their own reputations in order to sponsor a mentoree.

◆ Mentors model various aspects of leadership functions so as to challenge mentorees to move toward them.

◆ Mentors direct mentorees to needed resources that will further develop them.

◆ Mentors co-minister with mentorees, in order to increase their confidence, status, and credibility (Stanley and Clinton, *Connecting,* 1992:38).

### Finishing Well — from Moses to Timothy

To end well, we must not get too wrapped up in our own indispensability. Humility is the key to finishing well and passing the torch on to our successors.

One of the keys to successful leadership transition is to learn to hold our positions loosely. The tighter the grip, the more pride and the harder it becomes at any stage to let go. A loose grip is a humble grip, an attitude that knows our finitude and dispensability. People follow leaders for many reasons. But when that leader's time is done, they quite naturally transfer their loyalty to the next generation.

The Scriptures are filled with good examples of successful leadership transition based on the concept of humility and an understanding of one's own finitude. A few examples will set the stage for application.

*Moses and Joshua.* One of the great examples of a successful leadership transfer is Moses and Joshua, as the mantle was passed in Deuteronomy 34. For forty years Moses looked forward to finally taking his people into the Promised Land. But it was not to be. His successor, Joshua, would be the man to fulfill Moses' dream. In fact, the day before he died Moses was shown the Promised Land and told that his descendants would possess it — but he would never set foot in it: "I have let you see it with your eyes, but you will not cross over into it" (Deut. 34:4).

How did Moses handle the truth that his successor would

have greater success than he, and that Joshua would actually fulfill the objectives Moses himself had sought after for forty years? He handled it with godly grace and dignity:

> Now Joshua son of Nun was filled with the spirit of wisdom because Moses had laid his hands on him. So the Israelites listened to him and did what the Lord had commanded Moses (Deut. 34:9).

The plan worked, the transition was smooth, and the followers immediately transferred their allegiance to Joshua, because his predecessor had in humility placed his hands on Joshua and prayed for God's blessing on his leadership. That is leadership maturity in the final hour, when it probably counts the most.

*Jesus and the Twelve.* The entire leadership style of Jesus in His three years of active ministry was to find, select, and train His twelve successors. By the time of the Crucifixion, Christianity was only a small band of followers. Jesus set the pattern for what we call discipleship when He charged them to go and fulfill what He had begun:

> A new command I give to you: Love one another. As I have loved you, so you must love one another (John 13:34).

> Again Jesus said, "Peace be with you! As the Father has sent Me, I am sending you" (John 20:21).

> Therefore go and make disciples of all nations, baptizing them in the name of the Father and of the Son and of the Holy Spirit, and teaching them to obey everything I have commanded you (Matt. 28:19-20).

Jesus did not develop Christianity into a worldwide movement, but His early followers did. He chose not to accomplish His will without those who came after Him. In the same way, our successors will most likely be the ones to finish what we start.

***Paul and Timothy.*** I don't know any place in the New Testament that depicts the development of future leadership—our successors—more clearly than in 2 Timothy chapter 2, where Paul charges Timothy, his chief successor, to carry on his work, and to make sure that he in turn finds his own successors:

> And the things you have heard me say in the presence of many witnesses entrust to reliable men who will also be qualified to teach others (v. 2).

To survive and grow, a movement such as the Christian faith must be at least four-deep: Paul mentored Timothy, who was in turn asked to mentor others, who would still mentor others—four layers of successors, who indeed did spread the infant movement, eventually to every continent.

Success without successors is like a childless couple; the future of the family is cut off. In organizational life, a leader who fails to identify and develop his successor stalls the future effectiveness of the organization and hinders the fulfillment of its purposes.

## POWERPOINTS

If you're convinced by now that you need to develop your successors and, in due time, make way for them with humility, here are some ways to tackle those hard barriers to graceful transition:

***Regarding job security.*** What will you do and where will you go next? A leader who is a true servant of the organization will put the group's needs before his or her own. If it's time to go, then step out by faith and go. Look for another organization that can use your help. Trust God to care for your needs — even that big need for a new role. I have seen many examples of folks who have done this only to find that the leap turned into a great adventure.

***Regarding resistance to change.*** Everyone gets comfortable with familiar surroundings and regular routines. It is only human to resist drastic change. But growth comes from change. There's a woman who has worked in leadership for us in Hong Kong for twenty-five years. She recently decided she needed a change of venue, and is looking for a new assignment for her last decade before retirement. I applaud her sense of faith and her willingness to leap out in this change — for she is by nature a very orderly and routine-loving person. The change is not easy, but she knows it is right and best.

***Regarding fear of retirement.*** This is a problem as old as work itself. There are many good books and seminars out to help people deal with this major life transition. You owe it to yourself and to your organization, as well as your family, to get ready for retirement. Like airplanes that are mothballed out of service, a retiree with no plans for useful activity will soon fall apart.

***Regarding your self-worth.*** The normal adult (especially male) gains the greatest portion of his identity from the job. As we have seen this is especially true of workaholics. So what is the answer? Get a life! Find interests outside of work. Find fulfillment and worth in hobbies, sports (doing, not watching!), your spouse, children, and community organizations. Get more involved at your church. I've known men and women who eventually found new careers through seeking outside interests. Just this past weekend I was in a home of friends in San Jose, California. The woman, who is past retirement age, learned about four years ago that she has a professional gift in painting. Now she paints as a new career and sells her work in galleries throughout the Bay Area. How did it happen? A friend dragged her to her first art class four years ago, kicking and screaming!

***Regarding a lack of confidence in a successor.*** Many leaders fall into the trap of having no confidence that anyone else will do "as good a job as I can do." There is some justification for such a feeling. Your successor will not start out knowing as much as you know, or have as much experience as you have. But don't forget how things were when *you* were the young upstart. Have faith in the next generation, and come to grips with your own dispensability. The best way to make the transition out of a position of leadership is to make yourself psychologically ready for it long before it happens. Remember, you will do more damage to your organization by staying too long than by leaving too early.

***Regarding your love for the people and the job.*** This is perhaps the most emotional of all the reasons for hanging on. We love our work and we don't want to leave it. You love your children yet have to let them go out of the nest so they can sprout their own wings of independence. In the same way you owe it to the organization to let go when the time comes, giving them space to grow without your leadership control. The best defense against depression in this arena is a good offense: Find something else to replace that which took so much place in your life.

***Regarding your loss of investment.*** CEOs, senior pastors, and founders invest huge amounts of emotional, psychological, and personal effort into building their corporations. It is an investment that is hard to let go of. If you honestly trust the new generation of leadership, then you can relax and consider your time of leadership as the groundwork for the successful growth of the organization beyond your own direct involvement. You have not lost an investment, you have made a substantial contribution in the life of a movement that will succeed in the future because of your help.

***Mentoring constellations.*** Take some time to reflect on your mentoring constellations. Read the following questions and make your own mentoring list:

- ☑ Who are the people who challenge me? To whom do I look for stimulation to be my best and do my best?
- ☑ Who are the "men" or "women" I am developing to take my place when it is my turn to pass the torch?
- ☑ Who are my external peer mentors, who are basically on my level and in whom I find great stimulation and encouragement?
- ☑ Who are my internal peer mentors, those colleagues within my own organization through whom I find encouragement and stimulation to be and do my best?

***On the role of boards of directors.*** One final word, concerning boards of directors. In the issue of successors in leadership, it is imperative that the board takes a strong role in helping present leaders make the transition out as gracefully as possible. In fact, in no area of corporate or church life is there a stronger place to argue for a strong board than in the matter of transition.

A board of directors is charged with the ultimate oversight of the organization. At times a board will have to step in when the older leader is not willing to leave. I can think of two vivid examples of organizations that were at opposite ends of the spectrum in a situation like this. In one case, a weak board had no courage to stand up to the powerful leader who had long outlived his usefulness. So that leader stayed and stayed, and it put the organization years behind in their ability to be "state-of-the-art" in their niche. There was a vacuum of leadership at the helm and no one was able to fix the problem—from the bottom up or from the top down.

In another case, involving a similar type of organization and situation, the board was strong enough to call in consultants, determine that it was time for the founder to move on, and ultimately to call for his resignation. The process was done with love and firmness. It was painful but it was effective. A new leader was brought up from the ranks, and that leader has since taken the group to great new heights of ministry. Everyone still appreciates the founder and former CEO, recognizing that he had made his contribution in the founding stages of development.

The board of directors must be the first to transfer loyalty to a new leader, and to take a strong role in supporting this new man or woman in his or her new assignment. The people within the organization will follow the lead of the board.

Leadership is a high calling and a great privilege. Those of us who are tapped on the shoulders to lead must do so with an open hand. From our very first day on the job we need to keep in mind that day down the road when with humility we will have to pass the torch to our successor. And how we pass that torch might just be the ultimate measure of our leadership success.

One of the great mentors in my life is my father-in-law, Mark Bubeck. He recently passed the milestone of age 65 and wrote this poem as he reflected on the passing of the torch from his generation to mine:

## WATCHING THE TORCH PASS
### by Mark I. Bubeck

Power with men—It has much appeal,
Can't measure its length 'cause it's mostly the feel;
It's the honor, the praise, the not being left out,
It's others looking to you as the one with the clout;
It's so easy to swell and to hallow the pride,
So hard to claim meekness and remain humble inside;
Accolades keep coming and you're running to win,
It all seems so right—so distant from sin;

But the glory fades fast with its hue and its cry,
You're just George or you're Mary, whose life has passed by;
The memories remain there, but who wants to listen?
And those really knowing are mostly now missin';

Time passes swiftly! It roars down the pike,
Age swirls around you like floods through the dike;
Values change quickly in such pressings of time;
It's not really prestige or what ladder you climb,
It's the honor of God whom soon you will face;
It's the gold through the fire that produces true riches;
It's the eye salve to scratch where each hurting soul itches;

It's white clothing that covers our nakedness and shame
It's buying from Christ—not the extent of your fame,
That produces rewards that are worthy of praise,
To Him be the glory in an eternity of days;
It's the souls God has added through your witness and life,

Multiplying now 'midst Satan's hatred and strife,
Partners forever in the Gospel's Good News!
A body portrait of people in all colors and hues;
"Well done, faithful servant! Now enter your rest,
For you, chosen one, I've reserved what is best!"

# Failure to Focus
# on the Future
### *Prepare Yourself,*
### *It's Later than You Think*

▶ The future is rushing at us at breakneck speed.

▶ A leader's concentration must not be on the past nor on the present, but on the future.

▶ Vision is an effective leader's chief preoccupation.

▶ Organizations are reinvented with new generations of dreamers.

If it works, it's obsolete." These words from a futurist sent a chill down my spine. But if leadership is about the future, then the worst thing a leader can do is fear that future. Our present methods are already obsolete, so we constantly refine, improve, listen, and learn. Others may fear, but he or she who leads must boldly face the future.

Consider this letter of caution written in 1829 by future President Martin Van Buren to President Andrew Jackson, cautioning him to put the brakes on the future:

January 31, 1829

To: President Jackson

The canal system of this country is being threatened by the spread of a new form of transportation known as "railroads." The federal government must preserve the canals for the following reasons:

**One.** If canal boats are supplanted by "railroads," serious unemployment will result. Captains, cooks, drivers, hostlers, repairmen and lock tenders will be left without means of livelihood, not to mention the numerous farmers now employed in growing hay for horses.

*Two.* Boat builders would suffer and towline, whip and harness makers would be left destitute.

*Three.* Canal boats are absolutely essential to the defense of the United States. In the event of the expected trouble with England, the Erie Canal would be the only means by which we could ever move the supplies so vital to waging modern war.

As you may well know, Mr. President, "railroad" carriages are pulled at the enormous speed of 15 miles per hour by "engines" which, in addition to endangering life and limb of passengers, roar and snort their way through the countryside, setting fire to crops, scaring the livestock and frightening women and children. The Almighty certainly never intended that people should travel at such breakneck speed.

> Martin Van Buren
> Governor of New York
>
> (Quoted in "No Growth,"
> *The American Spectator,* Jan. 1984)

In 1829, 15 miles per hour was breakneck speed! As I write this page I am cruising at 34,000 feet above the earth at a speed of 475 miles per hour, comfortably sipping my coffee and typing on a notebook computer. Poor Martin would have a heart attack if he were still with us!

At Yellowstone last summer I saw a vivid illustration of the power of the future. There we were, standing at the crest of the Lower Falls of Yellowstone, the water rushing over the falls by the millions of gallons raging and roaring with an unbelievable power—a power that mankind tames only with great effort. And I thought, *that water is the future. It comes with such power and nothing can stop it.*

The future is rushing toward us and past us with an awesome power that no man can stop, any more than I can stop that raging torrent at Yellowstone.

## The Future Is Coming!

The future is approaching at lightning speed. In 1829 it came fifteen miles per hour. Today it rushes toward us in quantum leaps. With that future comes changes of earthquake proportions in how we do whatever we do. Cutting-edge leaders are completely rethinking the nature of organizations and the nature of leadership for the world of tomorrow.

Workers in our organizations are demanding to participate in decisions that are affecting their lives. I sense this more and more as a younger, different kind of workforce fills our ranks. No longer are workers willing to just blindly accept whatever comes down from the top. The democratization of organizations is threatening the very survival of many more traditional organizations. This democratization is forcing us to rethink our very understanding of the role of leaders and leadership, and how we structure organizations.

I mentioned these fundamental shifts in the chapters on "The Top-down Attitude" and "Dictatorship in Decision-making." But they have very much to do with the future as well.

We are seeing more and more of a trend toward flat organizations. Fewer people believe the centralized institutional approaches have the necessary wisdom or capability to generate progress.

The new generations, the baby boomers and busters, have lost confidence in the hierarchical processes of government, church, education, and business. Younger people are just not interested in investing their lives in the maintenance or fostering of institutional structures. They want to go where the action is, they want to make a difference, they want to work in flat organizations, *and they want to be in control of their destinies.* The new generations insist on participation in a networking relationship throughout their organization. They prefer a highly decentralized, grassroots approach to problem-solving.

## The Leader's Job Is the Future

"A leader is one who sees more than others see, who sees farther than others see, and who sees before others do."

*—Leroy Eims,*
Be the Leader You Were Meant to Be, *1975:55*

"Stay one step ahead of your people and you are called a leader. Stay ten steps ahead of your people and you are called a martyr!"

*(Source unknown)*

"Leaders are pioneers. They are people who venture into unexplored territory. They guide us to new and often unfamiliar destinations. People who take the lead are the foot soldiers in the campaigns for change . . . the unique reason for having leaders—their differentiating function—is to move us forward. Leaders get us going someplace."

*—Kouzes and Posner,*
The Leadership Challenge, *1988:32*

"Leadership is seeing the consequences of our actions further in the future than those around us can."

*—Bill Gothard*

## One Thing Is Constant: Change

When I was asked recently by my board of directors what is my greatest fear for our organization, it did not take me long to come up with an answer. "My greatest fear is that we become irrelevant and obsolete." I don't want us to hand our phonograph records to a CD generation, or show home movies to a world that is glued to their VCRs.

Change is inevitable; not to change is a sure sign of imminent extinction. Why do you think the dinosaur no longer roams the earth? It could not change as the climate of the earth around it changed. Leaders who don't change with

the changing climate of our future world will, like the dino-
saurs, find themselves only a museum attraction.

By nature we resist change. Most of us find it hard to see
new trends developing in our chosen fields. People are
quick to criticize innovations, because the changes frighten
them. The effective leader has to help his or her followers
feel good about the changes that lie ahead. I have to let my
people know that they can trust me to take care of them —
that I won't lead them to a dead end.

Once people said that cars would never replace the horse
and carriage. Others said that the light bulb wasn't really
better than the kerosene lamp. Then there are the naysayers who said that movies could never entertain like
vaudeville could. On the heels of that negative attitude
came the condemnation of television, which people were
sure would never supplant radio as the primary source of
entertainment.

When Alexander Graham Bell invented the telephone,
people laughed him out of town. Certainly people were not
ready for such an instrument, whereby people could talk to
one another through a wire over great distances! Leaders
have to lead into the future despite the naysayers and oppo-
sition.

### Dreamers and Visions
As I have mentioned, one of my very first jobs as a teenager
was as a busboy at a local Big Boy restaurant in my home
town of Huntsville, Alabama. Why did I work at that restaurant? One reason was to make money. And of course I got
paid by the hour.

Today I don't get paid by the hour, I get paid for results.
And I don't work today for the purpose of a paycheck. I like
to think that my main drive is to make a difference and to
have an impact on the future of my organization. I get paid
to lead us into the future. I couldn't have cared less about
the future of that Big Boy restaurant back in the 1960s.

Leaders are paid to be a dreamers. In fact the higher you

---

### Vision

"To choose a direction, a leader must first have developed a mental image of a possible and desirable future state of the organization. This image, which we call a vision, may be as vague as a dream or as precise as a goal or mission statement. The critical point is that a vision articulates a view of a realistic, credible, attractive future for the organization, a condition that is better in some important ways than what now exists."

*—Warren Bennis & Burt Nanus,*
Leaders, *1985:89*

"Vision for ministry is a clear mental image of a preferable future imparted by God to His chosen servants and is based upon an accurate understanding of God, self, and circumstances."

*—George Barna,*
The Power of Vision, *1992:28*

"There is no more powerful engine driving an organization toward excellence and long-range success than an attractive, worthwhile, achievable vision for the future, widely shared."

*—Burt Nanus,*
Visionary Leadership, *1992:3*

---

go in leadership, the more your work is about the future. I have very little influence on what is going to happen in my organization over the next six months, but I am making daily decisions that could have a profound impact on us one and five years down the road.

Some may ask in frustration, "How can I drain the swamp—how can I plan for the future—when I'm up to my neck in alligators?" The tyranny of the urgent always fights against our planning and thinking time, but if we don't make the time to plan for the future we will be its victims. We will develop a style of reactionary leadership. What is needed is proactive leadership that anticipates the future.

Proactive leaders are the leaders who have the most profound impact on the world. One such visionary leader was Walt Disney. Has anyone in North America not been influenced by this dreamer? Listen to his portrayal of the future, before the ground was broken for Disneyland in Anaheim:

> The idea of Disneyland is a simple one. It will be a place for people to find happiness and knowledge. It will be a place for parents and children to spend pleasant times in one another's company: A place for teachers and pupils to discover great ways of understanding and education. Here the older generation can recapture the nostalgia of days gone by, and the younger generation can savor the challenge of the future. Here will be the wonders of nature and man for all to see and understand. Disneyland will be based upon and dedicated to the ideals, the dreams, and hard facts that have created America. And it will be uniquely equipped to dramatize these dreams and facts and send them forth as a source of courage and inspiration to all the world.
>
> Disneyland will be something of a fair, an exhibition, a playground, a community center, a museum of living facts, and a showplace of beauty and magic. It will be filled with the accomplishments, the joys and hopes of the world we live in. And it will remind us and show us how to make those wonders part of our lives (B. Thomas, *Walt Disney: An American Tradition,* 1976:246).

Leadership must be always devoting itself to the issue of goals and strategies: Where are we going next, and why are we going there? Managers ask *how,* leaders ask *where* and *why?* We need organizations today that have this balanced dose of visionary leadership and effective management.

"We are more in need of a vision or destination and a compass (a set of principles or directions) and less in need of a road map," says Stephen Covey in *The Seven Habits of Highly Effective People.* Covey clarifies the difference in management and leadership when he says, "management is efficiency in climbing the ladder of success; leadership determines whether the ladder is leaning against the right wall" (Covey, 1991:101).

### Becoming a Learning Organization

While I was jogging recently in Wheaton, I could not help but stop in front of a house that had a square marble stone with a brass marker in its front yard. It caught my eye as unusual — a stone marker in a front yard? The house looked a bit eccentric — not your run-of-the-mill suburban home. On the marker were these words: *On This Spot in 1897 Nothing Happened.* I ran off feeling foolish for being taken for a ride. It would not surprise me if someone was watching from a window to see how I reacted.

> **Dreamers**
>
> **All men dream;**
> **but not equally.**
> **Those who dream**
> **by night in the**
> **dusty recesses**
> **of their minds**
> **Awake to find**
> **that it was vanity;**
> **But the dreamers**
> **of day are**
> **dangerous men,**
> **That they may act**
> **their dreams with**
> **open eyes to make**
> **it possible.**
>
> *T.E. Lawrence*
> *— Bennis & Nanus,*
> *Leaders, 1985:27*

As I jogged on, the truth of that marker hit me. My greatest fear for the future of the organization I lead is that it would be said, "after their 50th anniversary — nothing happened."

Whether we like it or not, we are in the midst of a paradigm revolution. Things are changing dramatically on the economic, technological, sociological, generational, and spiritual fronts. If we don't flex in our response to the changes external to us, we will become obsolete. The great opportunities of tomorrow will be seized by the younger, more aggressive groups who do respond. They may not do things the

> "My interest is in the future because I am going to spend the rest of my life there."
>
> — *Charles F. Kettering*

way we "think it ought to be done," but the reality of the matter is that they will be used despite themselves to get things done.

There are two ways to approach the future: *as learners, or as closed experts.* The opposite of the learner is the "know-it-all." This type of management has the attitude that they have mastered their trade. With rock-solid policies and procedures built on years of experiences and tradition, why should they change? The old way is not only the best way, but really the only way.

This is what I call the "pro" attitude: "We're the pros at this; others can look to us and see how it ought to be done." Christian organizations have the added paralysis of hiding behind their spiritual views — *theologizing their methodology.* The years of organizational tradition become a sacred cow that cannot and should not be tampered with — after all, it was created by our spiritual forefathers, who were led by God to create the organization we now inherit.

The most vivid story I know of a group that dominated the world in their industry and then became obsolete almost overnight is the Swiss watch industry. As we have seen, in the mid 1970s the Swiss made 85 percent of all watches sold in the world. By the mid 1980s they had laid off 25,000 watchmakers and were down to 15 percent of the world market. A simple new development, invented by a Swiss watchmaker but rejected by his institutional superiors, the quartz movement, redefined what the world thinks and expects of watches. The old watchmakers just didn't think the quartz was really a watch, because it had no mainspring and no knob to wind it up. The world changed, they remained the same, and the rest is history. Upstarts Seiko of Japan and Texas Instruments of Dallas saw the future and are now at the center of the watchmaking industry.

In *Changing the Essence,* Richard Beckhard and Wendy Pritchard speak of this issue that plagues all older traditional organizations:

> The assumptions that guided organizations in the past were, (1) that they could control their own destinies and, (2) that they operated in a relatively stable and predictable environment (Beckhard & Pritchard, 1992:2).

Beckhard and Pritchard call the changes in the external environments in which we must work "whitewater" turbulence: explosion of technology, changes in the political landscape, new relationships between the First and Third Worlds, worldwide changes in social values, the role of women, and the changing balance of financial wealth in the world (1992:1).

In our own organization I see the need for change. Just because God used us in the past is no guarantee that He will use us in the future. I am not saying that there's anything deadly wrong with us. The problem is that the world outside is changing; the international community we want to touch is changing; our new workforce is different, with different expectations; and our donor base is changing dramatically. All across the United States, churches are thinking differently about financial priorities. And the peoples in the nations we serve are thinking differently about our relationships to them.

### Faith and the Future

The future is coming. "When all else is lost, the future still remains," remarked Christian Nestell Bovee. The Bible has a lot to say about the future, in fact it is a book for futurists. Whole books of the Bible are devoted to the future in the form of divine prophecies—books like Daniel, Isaiah, and many of the minor prophets. In the New Testament, the Book of Revelation is devoted to an unfolding of what the future will hold as the Creator wraps up history as we know it.

I have read many books about the future, written by futurists. I enjoy them, but I read them with skepticism. Futurists do have the ability to predict trends based on solid scientific analysis. But they cannot know the future any more than astrologers can know it. The Bible is clear that no man or woman on earth knows the future:

Since no man knows the future, who can tell him what is to come? (Ecc. 8:7)

If you are the kind of person who tends to fear the future, then find comfort in the promises of God for His people. The Bible is very encouraging about the long-term future:

Let this be written for a future generation, that a people not yet created may praise the Lord (Ps. 102:18).

"For I know the plans I have for you," declares the Lord, "plans to prosper you and not to harm you, plans to give you hope and a future" (Jer. 29:11).

Since we are nearing the end of our look at the top ten mistakes leaders make, let's wrap things up with one final word about the future. Consider it a final caution. When the disciples met with Jesus after the Resurrection they were anxious about the future. In fact they were hoping that He was about to restore creation and usher in His kingdom. He gently rebuked them with a reminder that He is in control of the future, and that their job was to get to work sharing the Good News of salvation in His name.

He said to them: "It is not for you to know the times or dates the Father has set by His own authority. But you will receive power when the Holy Spirit comes on you; and you will be My witnesses in Jerusalem, and in all Judea and Samaria, and to the ends of the earth" (Acts 1:7-8).

Our highest task is to spead the news of Christ's coming. *His* job is to take care of the future. When all the nations have heard (Matt. 24:14) then He will bring to earth His promised, glorious future.

## POWERPOINTS

Creating vision and direction toward the future is one of the primary tasks of leadership. The leader is responsible to take the lead in planning for the future. He or she must lead the team in developing organizational goals, plans, and strategies that flow out of a crisp purpose or vision statement.

Notice I include "the team" in this. As we have seen, people throughout the organization are shareholders in the group, and want a say in planning for the future. The leaders who surround the head person should be an integral part in shaping vision and making plans. When the team has a stake in goal formation, they have a vested interest in goal ownership and in seeing these goals fulfilled.

Here is some concrete advice about building for the future:

*Set aside time to think about the future.* At least quarterly, I get away for a whole day just to reflect on the future, one to ten years out. It is important to take time away from the swamp, and forget about the alligators nipping at your neck! I find that my best time for future thinking is out of the office — in fact that is a requirement for me. Keep a "future file" in your computer, where you can store your dreams — away from the prying eyes of the bureaucrats and pragmatists. Above all, take time to dream.

***Perform a "vision audit."*** The first step in the right direction is a healthy understanding of your present position. Take the time to ask insiders and outsiders how they feel about the strengths and weaknesses of your organization. Perform a "vision audit" where you send out questionnaires and ask for honest feedback. Then gather the respondents together in small focus groups to discuss their feedback. Learning organizations are not afraid to hear the truth. Six of the most important questions to ask are:

a.   What are the strengths of our group?
b.   What are our greatest weaknesses?
c.   What should be our highest priorities?
d.   What do we do well?
e.   What do we do poorly?
f.   What barriers do we need to remove to fundamentally enhance our effectiveness for the future?

***Develop a fresh vision statement.*** Even if your organization is 50 or 100 years old, new times require fresh expressions of the group's passion. Some call them *purpose* statements, but I prefer the term *vision* because it seems fresher and more animated. Burt Nanus, in *Visionary Leadership,* defines vision as simply, " . . . a realistic, credible, attractive future for your organization. Selecting and articulating the right vision, this powerful idea is the toughest task and the truest test of great leadership" (Nanus, 1992:16, 28–29).

He goes on to state that, "powerful and transforming visions always tend to have the following special properties:

a.   They are appropriate for the organization and the time.
b.   They set standards of excellence and reflect high ideals.

c. They clarify purpose and direction.
d. They inspire enthusiasm and encourage commitment.
e. They are well-articulated and easily understood.
f. They reflect the uniqueness of the organization.
g. They are ambitious.

***Get together and set short- and long-term strategic goals.*** It is important to have a set of flexible, changing long- and short-term goals. I prefer to do this as a two-level process.

> *Annual goals for the organization:* I work with my leadership team to come up with an annual theme for each year and the goals we hope to accomplish in that year.

> *Quarterly goals for departments:* Most people seem to work best if you help them organize for the next quarterly time frame. Help them work through your expectations of them for the coming three months.

One final piece of advice on goal-setting: When you put together a set of goals for your mission, they should be SMART goals:

S — specific
M — measurable
A — attainable
R — relevant
T — trackable

***Concentrate and eliminate.*** Lyle Schaller observes that most churches are ineffective not because they do too little but because they attempt too much. The German poet Goethe put it this way: *The key to life is concentration and elimination.* Leadership must give itself to articulating a clear purpose statement and set of corporate goals that the top leadership can sign off on. Then the organization can focus and concentrate its resources on doing specifically what it was raised up to do, instead of dissipating energies by dabbling in a little bit of everything.

Not a week goes by that I am not confronted with another great opportunity that our organization should "jump on board with." After my initial excitement, I sit back and ask myself: *How does this square with what God has called us to do in the world?* If it is not going to lead to the fulfillment of our basic goals, we should not get involved.

Here is the same idea from management guru Peter Drucker:

Concentration is the key to economic results. No other principle of effectiveness is violated as constantly today as the basic principle of concentration. . . . Our motto seems to be, "Let's do a little bit of everything."

***Read all about it.*** Take time to read books about future trends by experts in your field. A number of writers spend their energies studying trends that affect all of us no matter what our endeavor. Some excellent sources of help are:

*Future Edge,* Joel Barker (William Morrow, 1992): The best book out on the concept of paradigm revolutions and paradigm pioneers.

*The Popcorn Report,* Faith Popcorn (Doubleday Currency, 1991): Popular trend watcher who makes interesting observations about developments in society that affect us all.

*Megatrends 2000,* John Naisbitt and Patricia Aburdene (William Morrow, 1990): Updated sequel for the '90s to *Megatrends,* the bestseller of the 1980s.

*Managing Workforce 2000,* David Jamieson and Julie O'Mara (Jossey-Bass, 1991): A comprehensive treatment of the changing nature of the workers who will fill the ranks of our organizations today and in the years to come.

*The Futurist,* a monthly periodical published by the World Futurists Society.

***Attempt and expect great things.*** I'm an eternal optimist. I know who holds the future and I know that I am eternally secure in His hands of control. Sure, bad things happen to good people, but ultimately history will unfold exactly as the Master has planned from the beginning. My passion is to *be all that I can be* in the full potential God has given me, and that I *do all that He wants me to do* in my short walk on this planet (see Phil. 3:12). For the organizations that I help lead, I expect of them no less than I expect from myself: Anticipate the future aggressively in the spirit of William Carey, who declared to his critics as he left for India 200 years ago, "Expect great things, attempt great things."

---

### Leadership Visions Are Snapshots of the Future

"A vision is a picture of a future state for the organization, a description of what it would like to be a number of years from now. It is a dynamic picture of the organization in the future, as seen by its leadership. It is more than a dream or set of hopes, because top management is demonstrably committed to its realization: it is a commitment."
— *Richard Beckhard & Wendy Pritchard,*
Changing the Essence, *1992:25*

"I am a dreamer. Some men see things as they are, and ask why; I dream of things that never were, and ask why not?"
— *George Bernard Shaw*

---

# REFERENCES CITED

Autry, James A.
    1991    *Love and Profit.* New York: William Morrow. Used with permission.

Barker, Joel
    1992    *Future Edge.* New York: William Morrow. Used with permission.

Barna, George
    1992    *The Power of Vision.* Ventura, Calif.: Regal Books.

Beckhard, Richard and Wendy Pritchard
    1992    *Changing the Essence.* San Francisco: Jossey-Bass. Used with permission.

Bennis, Warren
    1989    *On Becoming a Leader.* New York: Addison-Wesley.

Bennis, Warren and Burt Nanus
    1985    *Leaders: The Strategies for Taking Charge.* New York: HarperCollins, Inc. Used with permission.

Bradford, Lawrence J. and Claire Raines
    1992    *Twenty-something.* New York: Master Media. Used with permission.

Bubeck, Mark I.
    1993    "Watching the Torch Pass," unpublished poem. Used with permission.

Covey, Stephen
    1991    *The Seven Habits of Highly Effective People.* New York: Simon & Schuster.

DePree, Max
    1989      *Leadership Is an Art.* Copyright © 1987 by
              Max DePree. Used by permission of Double-
              day, a division of Bantam Doubleday Dell
              Publishing Group, Inc.

Drucker, Peter
    1990      *Managing the Non-Profit Organization.* New
              York: Harper Collins.

Eims, Leroy
    1975      *Be the Leader You Were Meant to Be.* Whea-
              ton, Ill.: Victor Books.

Erwin, Gayle
    1988      *The Jesus Style.* Waco: Word Books.

Greenleaf, Robert K.
    1977      *Servant Leadership.* New York: Paulist Press.

Hersey, Paul and Ken Blanchard
    1982      *Management of Organizational Behavior: Uti-
              lizing Human Resources, 49.* Englewood Cliffs,
              N.J.: Prentice Hall. Used with permission.

Killman, Ralph
    1984      *Beyond the Quick Fix.* San Francisco: Jossey-
              Bass.

Kouzes, James and Barry Posner
    1988      *The Leadership Challenge.* San Francisco:
              Jossey-Bass. Used with permission.

Law, William
    1967      *A Serious Call to a Devout and Holy Life.*
              Lanham, Md.: Littlefield Adams and Co.

Maxwell, John
    1993      *Developing the Leader within You.* Nashville:
              Thomas Nelson. Used with permission of
              John Maxwell and INJOY.

McGregor, Douglas
   1985    *The Human Side of Enterprise.* New York:
           McGraw Hill.

Nanus, Burt
   1992    *Visionary Leadership.* San Francisco: Jossey-
           Bass.

Nouwen, Henri J.
   1974    *Out of Solitude.* Notre Dame: Ave Maria
           Press.

Peters, Tom
   1991    "Management Excellence," in The Business
           Journal. *Chicago Tribune.* Sept. 9, 1991.

Peters, Tom
   1992    *Liberation Management.* New York: Alfred
           Knopf.

Peters, Tom and Robert Waterman
   1982    *In Search of Excellence.* New York: Warner
           Books.

Reeves, R. Daniel
   1993    "Societal Shifts," in *Ministry Advantage.*
           May/June. Pasadena, Calif.: Charles E. Fuller
           Institute.

Rodgers, Buck and Irving M. Levey
   1987    *Getting the Best out of Yourself and Others.*
           New York: HarperCollins, Inc. Used with per-
           mission.

Sanders, J. Oswald
   1967    *Spiritual Leadership.* Chicago: Moody Press.

Sanny, Lorne
   1992    "Leadership," *The Business Ministry Journal.*
           July/August.

Shaw, George Bernard
   1972    *Man and Superman.* Baltimore: Penguin.

Stanley, Paul and J. Robert Clinton
    1992        *Connecting.* Colorado Springs: NavPress. Used with permission.

Thomas, B.
    1976        *Walt Disney: An American Tradition.* New York: Simon & Schuster.

Tichy, Noel and Stratford Sherman
    1993        *Control Your Destiny or Someone Else Will.* New York: Currency Doubleday.

Van Buren, Martin
    1984        "No Growth," in the *America Spectator.* Jan.